TWIST & TURN
OF FAITH

TWIST & TURN
OF FAITH

A True Story

ISHTAR

Library of Congress Control Number:		2017900236
ISBN:	Hardcover	978-1-5245-2132-5
	Softcover	978-1-5245-2131-8
	eBook	978-1-5245-2130-1

Print information available on the last page.

Rev. date: 01/05/2017

To order additional copies of this book, contact:
Xlibris
1-800-455-039
www.Xlibris.com.au
Orders@Xlibris.com.au
744901

CONTENTS

To my two sons, who have given me strength, happiness, and love through my life's journey. They are my first priority in life. I sacrificed a lot of my youth to give them what they needed in life as best I could.

Also to my father, who gave me unconditional love and support through all the hardships I faced growing up. I have the utmost love and respect for him.

INTRODUCTION

How it all began …

My objective and my goal in life is to teach people to never give up. We all serve a purpose on this earth, and we were strategically situated to become the people we are to serve a purpose. Some spend days, weeks, months, years, and even decades trying to discover what purpose they serve on this earth. Others sacrifice lifetimes and never discover it.

The point is, whether we realise it or not, we really do serve a purpose in this world and in this lifetime. The objective is to help others gain the strength for their journeys through life. An essential key to this is to always keep your eyes open. Recognise and identify signs throughout life to strengthen yourself and provide yourself with direction in life.

It has taken me about ten years to finally decide to write this book. I was waiting for a sign, a spiritual awakening from a higher spirit to guide me to the right path. What motivated me to tell my story are my sons, my youngest especially, and also my father, who I had a deep love and affection for. I'm hoping to leave a legacy for my sons—something special that I can leave behind when I'm no longer in this world. I want to document all my memories and all the obstacles and hardships I faced whilst growing up.

However, this is also a story of survival and how I found inner strength to face my fears and demons along the way. I made a choice to follow my own destiny, and it has led me to where I am today. It has also made me the person I am today: strong, independent, fearless, and spiritual.

Not everyone was born with a spiritual gift. Some have learnt to practise this by reading books or going to classes. My purpose is to guide true mediums to use their gift to help others in need of a spiritual awakening. The gift comes from within; it's not something that you can learn. If a person truly has a gift, he or she will be given signs through dreams, life experiences, and messengers from a higher power. God doesn't just come down to earth; he sends messengers, who are ordinary people like you and me, and he channels his thoughts through them like a vessel.

I truly believe in a higher spirit, in goodness, and that whatever you do in this lifetime will come back to you in a different way, one way or another. Whatever sacrifices we make for the good will come back in time. Patience is a virtue.

We are all equal in God's eyes. There are so many people who need guidance and direction in their lives because there are a lot of dilemmas people come across in their journeys—dilemmas such as confusion, emotional stress, financial difficulties, and other unexpected surprises that life has in store. My goal is to help people see that there is more to life than what they can see right in front of them.

Behind every door there is another dimension, another form of life. It's not just a black-and-white picture. People have strength they don't realise they have. Fear takes over, and it is a powerful emotion that stops them from moving forward and taking chances in life.

People who come to me have usually found themselves looking at a wall. My gift enables me to guide them to see the options behind that wall and what life has to offer them. I want to reach out to the people who have lost themselves and their souls in their journeys of life. Based on my own experiences growing up, I want people to realise that if I can make it, so can they. All they need is someone to guide them spiritually to make the right choices for themselves.

CHAPTER 1

THE BEGINNING

It was January 1960 in Mosul, Iraq, when my mother gave birth to me. I was born at home, with a midwife assisting my mother. My parents had struggled to conceive straight away when they got married. I was to be their miracle baby after five years of trying without any luck.

My parents lived with my grandparents on my father's side because, like other relatives who lived there with us, they could not afford to buy a house of their own. So there we were, eight of us crammed into a tiny mud house.

When I was born, everyone was elated, especially my grandmother. She could not believe she finally had a granddaughter. A year later, my parents separated. My mother went to live with her parents in Dohuk, which is north of Iraq, and left me behind in the care of my father's parents. Her own parents refused to let her take me with her under their roof. Their reason was that she got married without children, so she could only come back by herself.

My father was away at work as a building engineer, so he wasn't there most of the time. He was an intelligent man, even though he never studied at school. He was self-taught and learnt from his own initiative. He could read and write in Assyrian and

Arabic. My father was also taught to read and write in English by a generous English couple who were working as archaeologists in the north of Iraq.

My mother, on the other hand, was illiterate. She could only speak Assyrian. She could not read or write in Assyrian, Arabic, or English.

My father was working in Baghdad as a contractor for a Japanese company. My grandparents took on the responsibility of raising me as their own daughter. My grandfather was a retired war veteran from World Wars I and II. He had been presented with many medallions and also met King George VI. My grandfather was a very brave man, but he came back from the war a changed person. He was a heavy drinker, although he still had a pure and generous heart. He spoke seven languages: Arabic, Assyrian, Russian, German, English, French, and Italian.

My grandmother was his complete opposite. She was a typical housewife. She looked after the family while he was away for long periods of time. My grandmother had to learn to cope on her own and raise her children without their father around most of the time. She was beautiful, spiritual, loving, caring, and generous.

I loved my grandparents. They looked after me and made sure I had all the essentials. My parents had left me behind when I was one year old, so I thought my grandparents were actually my parents. They raised me until I was five years old.

My parents reunited in Baghdad while I was still living with my grandparents in Alqosh. My grandmother found out and took me back to them because she wanted them to take responsibility for their own daughter.

I vividly remember when my grandmother left to go to Baghdad. I didn't see her sneak out. She didn't even say goodbye. I was so upset; I was sick for three days because I was so attached to her. She was like my own mother. I didn't understand why she was gone, so I cried and slept under my bed.

When my grandmother gave me back to my parents, I felt so lost and confused. I felt like I was an orphan, because they were complete strangers to me. My father tried to make me accept that they were my parents, but I refused to believe it. That's when the horror started in my life.

My mother was a very hard woman who showed no emotion, affection, or love towards me. I never felt that she was proud that I was her daughter. She neglected me once I was back in their lives. She used to go to work for five hours and keep me locked up in the room because she didn't want anyone else looking after me. My mother didn't trust anyone. She thought that they could have bad influences on me and tell me things that she didn't want me to know.

I remember the room so vividly. It was like a prison cell. There was a bar window that looked over the roof of the house. I could hear children playing outside and other people walking and laughing. I couldn't understand why I was locked up and isolated from the world.

My mother used to leave me with a bottle of water so I wouldn't dehydrate. There was no toy, doll, television, or radio in that room, so I used my imagination to play with things that were already in there. I had a fantastic imagination. I used to play with a pair of my father's socks and my bottle of water and pretend that I was doing the laundry. I used to fall asleep and then repeat what I was doing. I did that to pass the time until my mother got home from work. I was lonely and isolated and felt the whole world's weight on my tiny shoulders.

I remember an incident that happened when I was five years old. While walking down the road, I found ten dinars. I didn't know what money was back then; I just picked it up because I loved the colour of it. I went home and fell asleep with the money in my hand. My mother found me sleeping and saw me holding something. She opened my hand and found the money.

My mother woke me up and asked me where I found it. I explained to her that I found it in the street and picked it up, not because it was money but because I was attracted to the colour. We used that money to buy food because my mother didn't have any. My father was away at work, so we were always tight on money and had a hard time making ends meet.

My mother used to blame me for everything that happened in her life. She always said that I brought bad luck when I was born. I was a curse. She believed that she and my father split up because of me. However, I found out later on that my father was an alcoholic. My mother told him to stop drinking, but he refused. He said that she couldn't tell him what to do and if she wasn't happy to go and leave him.

I have only good memories of my father. He used to spoil me and take me to the movies. He bought me my first black-and-white television; it was a Sanyo. I was so excited. I felt that I was special. All my neighbours in my village used to come and watch my television. My father tried to make sure that I felt loved by him, and at that time I really did. My mother complained that the television was too expensive, but my father argued that it was special for his daughter.

The transition from being with my grandparents and then suddenly being forced to live with my real parents was the most difficult time in my young life. I used to call my parents by their first names because they were strangers to me. The older I got, the harder my mother was on me.

My sister was born in 1965, the same year I moved back in with them in Baghdad. She was born at a hospital in that region. My mother spoilt her, which made me feel even more neglected and unwanted. She physically, verbally, mentally, and emotionally abused me.

I remember how much I loved going to school. For me, it was a way to forget what was going on at home. I had many friends who kept me going. It was my escape from all the horror I faced living at home. My mother would not let me go out anywhere; she never trusted me. She tried to control my life in every way possible.

I always looked forward to the holidays because my grandparents would come and visit me, and also check to see if I was all right. They used to stay at the house for weeks, and I remember feeling so excited. My grandmother would tell me stories, and I would rest my head on her chest so I could hear her heart beat. She used to tap my shoulder lovingly until I fell asleep in her warm embrace.

When my sister was born, I took on the responsibility of helping my mother look after the baby, as she had stopped working. At the age of five, I was forced to grow up quickly. Nine months after my sister was born, my mother gave birth to another baby girl. I didn't see my father much, because he was always away at work, so I was my mother's helping hand. At the age of six, I was helping my mother look after two babies under the age of two. Life for me got harder, as I was responsible for both of my sisters.

Two years after the third child was born, my mother got pregnant again with a baby girl. That child only survived three days before she passed on. She was not baptised, so my father carried her in a bag and buried her under a tree near our house. I remember feeling so sad, shocked, and helpless because I witnessed my mother giving birth to her and felt a connection with her straight away. Little did I know that tragedy would strike twice.

My mother got pregnant again soon after. I remember being in the same room and watching her giving birth. She gave birth to another daughter. My sister survived for three days and then passed on. This was a devastating time for our family.

Nine months after this tragedy, my mother gave birth again to a healthy baby girl. This time my sister, who was the fifth child, survived. I believe that the two tragic events before this were a curse. My mother wanted a baby boy so much, and she was never able to fulfil that wish.

Our whole family was so worried that the child would not survive. However, my sister beat the odds and grew up to be a healthy child. I had a special connection to this sister. I looked after her and made sure that she was safe and happy. She used to call me "mother." I remember my mother being jealous that her own daughter was calling me that because they didn't have the same connection.

So by the age of eleven, I was helping my mother look after three young children. I felt like I was a slave. I had lost my childhood, and I felt trapped. Little did I know that five years down the track, my mother would get pregnant again with another baby girl.

During this time, my father was at a mental institution, seeking psychological help for issues he had. He had become violent and lost a lot of his present memory. It was such a sad time for me and my family. I was so scared for him. I just wanted to be able to help him, but I didn't know how.

He broke the television he had bought me. However, he always regretted it and wanted to fix it. He could only remember the past, and so we knew something was wrong with him. My father stayed there for only two weeks and then left and resumed life as he knew it. Years later, we found out that he had a brain tumour.

When my father got better, my mother was pregnant for the last time. I waited outside to tell my father the news. He was not happy about it, because he so desperately wanted a son. My father wanted his family name to last forever. I decided at that time that I would always keep my father's name, even when I got married later on. My sister was only forty days old when I left to go to Greece to meet my fiancé.

CHAPTER 2

A CHILD'S VISIONS

It all started with a dream when I was eight years old. I didn't quite understand it, and so I told my mother straight away, because she was good in interpreting dreams that had underlying messages.

In our house, we had another family living with us. The mother was a widower whose husband passed away suddenly. He was an electrician by trade and was electrocuted while at work. My father was really good friends with this man, and so when the tragedy happened, he offered to help her and her five children. She lived with us along with three of her sons. Her other two children were not living with us because one had run away with a young Muslim Iraqi boy and the other had entered a convent to become a Christian nun.

I had a great connection with the middle son. We used to play together, fight together, and cry together. I really liked him, and I sensed that he liked me too. I can still remember what he looked like and smelt like. He was a handsome young boy—tall, dark-haired, strong-willed, with the most beautiful green eyes.

Like his father who had passed on, he too was fascinated by electricity and would play with power plugs. I remember my father catching him playing with the power plugs and telling him off. I thought it was funny every time he got into trouble.

I remember this dream so vividly, like it only happened yesterday. A thief came through the window and took that boy. In the dream, I was in the same room, and I was the only one there with him. I wanted to scream, but somehow I couldn't. I remember feeling so helpless because I wanted to protect him, but I couldn't, because it felt like I was being held back by a strong power. I woke up screaming and sweating. It felt so real because I could feel the pain in my heart.

My mother came to my side and asked me what happened. She gave me a glass of water to calm me down, and then I told her what I saw in my dream. My mother told me to say a prayer and then go back to sleep. I held on to my cross and started praying because I was so terrified. I could still see it in my thoughts and in my mind. The energy was so strong; I didn't understand what was happening to me.

The next day, I heard my mother talking to my father about my dream. She told my father that the dream wasn't a good sign; it represented the angel of death who came as a thief, who hides his identity. My mother told my father to keep an eye on the boy, because she was afraid that something would happen at home, as that young boy was fascinated with electricity. My father tried very hard to look out for him. I couldn't understand why I had that dream. I was terrified. I couldn't think of anything else but that dream.

A week after my dream, that boy tragically passed on. He was electrocuted at a railway. I remember that day clearly. He asked me if I wanted to go out and play with him because he had a kite that he wanted to test out. I had to refuse his invitation because I had to look after my younger sisters at home. Both my parents were at work, and so I had to take on the responsibility of looking after the family. I asked him not to go because I wanted him to stay at home with me to keep me company. He insisted that he was going out to fly his kite that he had made a few days before.

A few hours later, I noticed that there was a commotion outside. There were people crying and running around looking shocked. I decided to go outside and find out what was going on. One of the boys who was playing outside told me frantically that my friend had died at the railway that was situated near our house. I was numb; I couldn't believe what I was being told.

I found out later on the exact details of what happened that fateful day. My friend was out flying his kite at the railway with other boys from the neighbourhood. His kite got stuck between some power lines above a pole, and he couldn't get it out. The top of the pole was very high up, and the boys around him were daring him to go and get his kite. Being a strong-willed and mischievous young boy, my friend decided to climb up the pole and try to get his kite out.

As he was untangling his kite, he accidently touched the power lines and got electrocuted. The force of that threw him down, and his head landed on the railway line. He died instantly as the back of his skull exploded on the tracks.

The funeral happened straight after the accident. My father organised it and helped the boy's mother try to cope. It was a very sad time for me; to experience something like that as a young child is very traumatic. His accident kept playing over and over in my head. I started to see his face in my dreams. My mother started to get worried because she thought that he would try to take me in my dreams.

His mother was devastated, losing first her husband and then years later her son the same way. She mourned for a very long time; she had lost her will to live. Every time she looked at me, she would cry because she knew we were close. We would feel his presence in our house constantly. The electricity would play up every now and then.

My mother knew it was best if they left, because there were too many memories for them. My father helped her and her children move out to a house in another area. It was the best way for her and her family to move forward in life. As soon as they left, the energy problems left with them. Eventually, two years later, we moved out as well. The memories were too strong to forget.

CHAPTER 3

THE LOVE STORY: ASHUR AND ISHTAR

I was only fifteen years old when I met this man who I truly loved and adored. I was so happy at this stage, so full of energy. I was excited and childish, with butterflies in my stomach. It was a nice escape for me.

I had known this man from my childhood. We grew up together. I knew his whole family. His father was friends with my father, and in fact they grew up together. I was so young, so involved in study and school, that I wasn't even aware of boys and their intentions. I was so naive and clueless. I wasn't interested in this man; he wasn't my type at all.

Once I started school, this boy began to follow me to and from and around school—giving me funny looks, checking me out. I wondered what the story was with this guy. Everywhere I walked, he was right behind me.

One day I pulled aside his sister, who I was friends with, and asked her what his story was. Why did this young man keep following me? Why was he looking at me like that? I told her to tell him to stop following me, otherwise I would start throwing rocks at him when I saw him. His sister then began to tell me about how interested her brother was in me and how he'd asked her to speak with me to consider going out with him. She said he really wanted to be with me.

I kept saying no, and with her sales-pitch voice she pleaded with me to give him a chance, saying he was a very nice, genuine guy. I asked for her to give me some time to think about it, because this is not something I had done before. I had no idea what was going on or what to expect.

A few days later, this young lady approached me again, asking me what my thoughts were on the situation and whether I had considered giving this young man a chance at love. I agreed to give him a chance. I was very clear on one thing, however: "If he messes up, I'm out of there! I won't want to know anything about him or have anything to do with him."

We began to send letters to each other. When we would see each other, we only spoke very briefly, because we didn't want anybody in our families to know, particularly our parents. Only my sister and his sister had any idea what was going on. My younger sister who was only ten years old at the time would take my letters to him. She thought that he liked her because he would speak to her also, and she had a little crush on him too. It was all so sweet and innocent. I explained to my sister that he liked me and that was the reason we were writing each other letters, and that she was simply delivering these letters for us.

There were many romantic letters that went back and forth. The situation got more and more frustrating for him because he just couldn't wait to see me, and all he wanted to do was just talk to me in person. He asked me to meet him outside one night at a particular time. He told me he would be outside the window, and I would see him waving from the window, and I could go out on the roof and we could talk. I was so nervous and so very excited. I had butterflies in my stomach.

The houses that we lived in had flat roofs. In summer on hot nights, we would sleep on the roof. People would sit on their roof and eat, drink, and socialise. From the roof, there was a door that opened to a staircase that led to my bedroom upstairs. My parents' bedroom was downstairs, so they couldn't hear anything or take notice if there was any noise. It was very private.

One particular night I was supposed to meet him at one o'clock in the morning but I fell asleep and didn't meet with him. He tried and tried, knocking and looking through the window, and got scared. I was always punctual and never let him down, so he knew this was out of character for me. He was worried something may have happened to me.

Frustrated and worried, he felt he had no choice. He climbed up the poles on the back of the house, and with his friend's help he climbed up onto my roof. I was awakened, eyes wide open, pupils dilated, and frightened to the point where I was speechless. I was startled by a sudden chilly sensation and somebody next to me calling my name. "Ishtar, wake up."

It was so dark. I squinted trying to see who was in my room. By luck that night, the door that led to the roof happened to be open, and he had sneaked into my room. I began to ramble in my panicky anxious state, "Oh my God, how did you get in here? What have you done? There's going to be trouble tonight! If anybody hears us, they're going to kill us both!"

He turned to me and desperately said to me, "I had to see you. I just had to see you tonight. I thought something had happened to you! I was so worried!" It was so innocent. I had simply fallen asleep.

The friend that he was with who helped him climb up onto the roof and sneak into my house was a really lovely Kurdish guy who worked in a local bakery. He was also madly in love with a girl, and so for all of us, it was a very romantic time in our lives. We shared this together, and we all supported each other. My mother used to send me to his work to bring bread back, and he used to make me wait so I could see Ashur. All the names and abuse I used to get from my mother for returning back late, being degraded, belittled, and called names that a young girl had no idea about was all worth it just to see the love of my life.

Ashur and I began to make the roof encounters a more regular occurrence and a regular meeting point. I used to be so scared; I would shake and tremble virtually every time I saw him on the roof. I used to think that somebody would see him on the roof and think it was a thief and call the police. It frightened me each and every time. He was so careful, though, making sure that he was quiet and tactful in his approach. He was very good. I would laugh at how clever he was.

The door would be locked and he would be on the roof, and we would talk through the window when we met. The window had iron bars that we used to talk through. We shared the occasional innocent kiss through the bars of the window when he would leave, and if the door was ever unlocked, we would sit on the roof together and have deep and meaningful conversations for hours on end. It was summertime—romantic and full of warmth and love.

During the summer, my sister and I sometimes slept on the roof. He would come and lie down next to me on the roof, and we would stare at the stars and talk about what life would be like when we got married. We would plan our future and discuss what we would do with our lives together. We discussed all of our dreams and wishes for our future.

One night as we were talking, Ashur told me that he couldn't stay in the country and that he had to leave. If he stayed, he would have to go into the army, which was mandatory. I was scared that if he did go into the army he would get hurt or killed. It was so dangerous.

He told me that he had to escape, but not to worry because wherever he would go, he would find a way to get to me and have me meet him there. He told me not to worry and that he loved me. Our love was strong and would conquer anything.

I continued in school and kept studying. Ashur dropped out of school and went to find work so he could save money to make his great escape and start our new life together. He began working for a foreign-owned truck company. He was a very good driver and would travel interstate and over the border. One day he took me for a drive with him. I had told my mother that I was going to a friend's house that day. My mother knew this particular friend of mine, and she knew that we were very close friends. She trusted me and took my word for it. I was so frightened. He took me on a long drive; it felt as though we were driving for an eternity.

During all this time, Ashur was saving money and trying to arrange his passport to escape the country. His sister was living in Greece, where she had married a local man, and she was prepared to help in any way possible and have her brother join her. At this point, my aunty had lost her husband, and as a recent widow she didn't wish to stay in Iraq any longer. The memories were far too painful. She sold everything she owned and made her escape in search of change and a better life in Greece also.

I gave all of my aunt's details to Ashur and told him that she was there and he was welcome to contact her. She would send me letters and correspond with me, letting me know how he was. My aunty did send me letters over time reassuring me and telling me not to worry. She told me that he would look after me; he wanted to marry me. She wanted the best for me and was going to make sure I would get the treatment I deserved.

My heart was dark, heavy, and full of pain. The day he left was the saddest day of my life. I felt abandoned. We couldn't see each other that night. He couldn't leave the house, because he knew his parents would question where he was going. He had to keep a low profile until the following day, when they would drive him to the airport and he could make his swift getaway. I was full of sadness and sorrow.

I woke up very early for some strange reason and woke my sister up. I sent her to go to his house to see if he was still there. His friend came running in a manic state to me. He began to ramble in his panic asking where I'd been. He said that they came to see me the previous night, but they couldn't see me through the window, and that it made Ashur so sad. He turned me and said, "He wants to see you! He wants to say goodbye!"

His friend returned to Ashur and told him we had spoken. The next thing I knew, I heard the thumping of running footsteps up the pavement towards me. He came to find me to say goodbye. I cried like a baby saying goodbye to him; I just didn't want to let him go. He told me to stop crying. In the blur of my teary vision, I spotted a glisten in the sun. He presented me with a ring. "This is a promise from me and a reminder to you of our love. Every time you look at it, you can remember me." With that, he took off.

For weeks I was so sad and depressed. The love of my life had abandoned me. In the meantime, I had my mother on my case, continuously asking me what was wrong. Why was my face so down? Why was I sad? She just didn't know when to stop. I would get angry and upset with her. The more she would whinge and nag at me, the more upset I would get.

The verbal abuse continued from my mother, so I was now not only being abused emotionally by my mother but was trying to heal a broken heart at the same time. The only contact I had with Ashur were the letters from my aunty.

I had a neighbour who liked me at the same time. He knew about my relationship, and he knew that Ashur had left. He would try to persuade me and change my mind to see that Ashur was bad for me, and that if he loved me he wouldn't have abandoned me. This neighbour would send me love letters expressing his feelings for me—so innocent, so heart-set on marriage at fifteen years old, which was the normal thing in those days. I would write back telling him that he and I grew up together and were more like siblings. I didn't want him, I wanted Ashur. I asked him to stop sending me these letters.

Around this time, a lady we knew came to my father with her son to ask for my hand in marriage. My father turned her away and told her that I would marry whoever I chose to. He was not interested in a set-up or arranged marriage.

My uncle had seen the commotion and asked what was going on. I told him that they came to ask for my hand in marriage. My uncle laughed and told me there was no way I would marry that fool; he was no good for me. I knew this. Besides, I already had my true love.

My uncle was like my best friend. We were close in age, and we were very close friends. My uncle insisted that I deserved better than to settle for that boy.

My uncle told my mother off because she was behind the arranged marriage set-up. My mother insisted that I was old enough to get married and that I needed somebody to support me and to make money so that I could provide for the rest of my family. She only wanted me to marry him for money—and so that she would have one less mouth to feed.

Ashur had been living with his sister in Greece for almost a year. He spent a lot of time with my aunty and would write letters to me with her. While he was in Greece, he worked hard to save money.

During this time, his father went to visit Ashur and his sister. His father took him some money to help him out and also to help his sister buy furniture. His father was a great man, a chef by trade. He was extremely intelligent, kind, and warm-hearted—a truly beautiful person.

Ashur spoke to his father about me. He confided in his father and confessed his love for me and said that he wanted to marry me. He asked that his father return to Iraq, ask for my hand in marriage on his behalf, and hand me this letter.

His father returned and spoke to his wife about his son's request and proclamation of love for me. The wife refused and said that I was not suitable for their family. There was bickering back and forth and many a heated exchange of words regarding the matter between his parents. Ashur's mother still insisted and refused to give us her blessing for marriage. She insisted that we were too young and that it was not a good idea.

When Ashur heard about this in Greece, he contacted his parents and threatened them, saying that if they did not ask for my hand in marriage, he would return to Iraq and join the army. Knowing how dangerous the army was in Iraq and fully aware of the likelihood that he would be killed, they accepted his wishes.

Once his parents realised that they really had no choice in the matter, they went to visit my parents and ask for my hand in marriage. This was the first that my father had heard of our relationship, and of course suddenly all the pieces of the puzzle came together, and my parents realised what had been going on. This explained all of the strange behaviour.

My mother began instigating trouble and arguments with everybody around me. She was picking fights with my uncles, aunties, friends, everybody. She was so upset that she was the last to know about what was going on. She felt betrayed that nobody had told her.

Nobody was encouraging my choice to marry this man. The only person who was supportive was my father. He backed me up when everybody was making excuses and reasons for why I shouldn't be with Ashur. Nobody could or would give reasons why I should. My father defended me and told everybody that I was free to choose who I wanted to marry, and when they had daughters of their own they had the right to give their opinion. In this case, their opinion was not welcome.

My father sat down with me and spoke about my relationship with this man. I explained that we had realised we liked each other about a year ago, and that he had asked me to marry him and wanted me to leave with him. Surprisingly enough, my father agreed and insisted that I leave the country and go to Greece to be with Ashur. My father didn't want me to miss out on the opportunity of being able to live in another country.

Once upon a time, before my father got married, he'd had the opportunity with work to move to France. He was made an offer to work and live in Paris. It was a great-paying job, and he would've had a wonderful life in the city of love. He declined the offer and regretted it. He did not want me to make the same mistake and miss out on this opportunity. He insisted that he would help me leave.

Once my family accepted the request of my hand in marriage, both families got together and celebrated. Nobody knew who this man was who I was going to marry. His older brother was there and approached me and said, "Why are you marrying my brother? He's an idiot! I always loved you; I always wanted to be with you." I was shocked and tried to pick my jaw up off the floor. I had been hit with this bombshell that his brother was in fact in love with me.

Defensive and annoyed, I replied, "Excuse me, and how dare you! You never mentioned anything of the sort to me, and now all of a sudden you decide to confess your love to me?" I continued on my rant, "No thank you, I love Ashur. I want to be with him, and I will do anything I have to do be with this man. And don't ever speak about your brother that way!" Nothing more was said.

I became engaged to be married without my fiancé present. Everybody saw pictures of him, but of course nobody except my sister had ever met him or knew him. It was so difficult for my father to accept what was going on, having never met this man who he was giving his daughter to. However, he knew in his heart that he would be happy as long as I was happy. All my father ever sought was my happiness.

My father went and signed documentation for my passport, because I was underage to sign my own documentation. At the same time, his parents were leaving the country also. The time had come. I was about to leave everything and everybody I knew behind.

My favourite uncle, who was also my best friend, wanted to have festivities to celebrate my engagement and a going-away party for me. My parents refused; if any authorities were to find out what was going on, they would try to stop us. Everything had to be very quiet, low-key, and secretive. After all, I was escaping my country.

At six o'clock in the morning, I left for the airport. My sister was crying. Tears filled her little eyes and snowballed down her cheeks. She had a look of sombre sorrow on her face. It was so difficult to look at her and know I was leaving her behind. My sister pulled at my dress and begged me not to leave her.

My father was lying on his mattress in the lounge room where he usually slept. He greeted me, wished me good luck, and did not shed a tear. He looked at me and said with conviction and pride, "I wish you all the best, and I want you to be happy." I thanked him, swallowing a great big lump in my throat and fighting back what felt like a waterfall of tears. This was the most difficult time in my little life so far, leaving my beloved father behind.

I will never forget the look on his face when I left. No tears, no emotion; he simply smiled and wished me luck. "Have a wonderful life, and I will be there to join you soon."

Saying goodbye to my mother was a completely different experience. My mother turned to me bitterly and cursed at me. "I hope to God you go and never see anything good in your life. I hope that you will never be happy." I turned to her, politely thanked her, and walked away. Such a kind, warm goodbye from my mother.

I left with pride, my head held high. I showed no emotion, although I was deeply saddened by what I was about to do. As soon as I was out of their sight, I began to cry hysterically and scream. I was coming to the realisation that this was real. I was really leaving. What was I doing? There was no choice here. I had to go. I had to escape.

I took the plane with my aunty's mum because she was also traveling on the same plane with us who was also leaving with her family. We left on the same plane and arrived in Greece on the same day.

This was my new beginning …

CHAPTER 4

LIFE IN GREECE

We finally arrived at Athens airport. It was my future mother-in-law, all of her children, and myself; there were around seven or eight of us. We were all so excited to finally taste freedom. Ashur's mother was particularly excited and bought a bottle of alcohol when we arrived in Athens from the Duty-Free store to celebrate. We were all together in the airport waiting patiently for everybody's passport and bags to be checked one by one.

As a result of her excitement and while rummaging through her bags, Ashur's mother dropped the bottle of alcohol on the floor, and it shattered. The fumes from the alcohol were overwhelming. Airport security was scuffling like mad trying to get the mess cleaned up.

Once they had cleaned up the toxic alcohol spill, they discovered that there was something wrong with her passport. I wasn't even aware of what was going on through my excitement. I was dazed, looking around and through the glass barriers. I could see my Ashur waiting for me. I couldn't go anywhere because I had to wait for everybody to finalise their security check and go through the passport checkpoint.

Once the security staff realised that there was an issue with her passport, they took her into a separate room for questioning. In the meantime, I kept looking out through the glass, so close to freedom. People were tapping on the windows trying to capture the attention of their loved ones. My eyes caught Ashur's, and he came up to the window and placed his hands on the glass where mine were, as if to touch my hand through the glass. I couldn't wait to touch his hand for real. The anxiety and the wait was excruciating.

Ashur's brother and brother-in-law offered to go into the interview room to interpret for Ashur's mother. His sister was married to a German Greek man, tall in stature and build and quite intimidating to be in the presence of. He had striking blue eyes and broad shoulders, and he walked proud and so certain of himself. At first, the two men were denied access to the room; however, after much persuasion, they convinced security to allow them to assist.

Ashur came in with them and of course came straight over to me. He was hugging me and kissing me; he couldn't keep his hands off me. My aunty being overprotective of me, and of course I was so young, came straight over to us, slapped his hands off me, and told him not to touch me. She insisted on keeping us separate.

Ashur pulled faces at my aunty, was sarcastic, and teased her as if to say, "There's nothing you can do to stop me." The men went into the interview room and interpreted, and after a gruelling two-hour interrogation session, they finally released Ashur's mother and granted her a visa into the country.

Once she was allowed to leave, we all began our exciting journey to the cars that were pre-arranged to pick us up and take us to where we were going to be staying in this new country that we would now call home. As we were driving along, I found myself gazing out the window at the amazing scenery. I was in picturesque Greece. It was breathtaking. Simply beautiful. I felt freedom. I could taste the freedom. It was the most liberating feeling I had ever experienced.

Along the way, my aunty asked me about back home. She wanted to know how my father was. I explained his situation and health concerns. This made her sad; however, she needed to know what was going on back home with her family.

After a long drive, we arrived at Ashur's sister's house, where we met officially. I knew her from back home but had never really spoken to her. The extent of our conversation had never really gone beyond a basic hello prior to this point. I stayed there for a couple of hours and then headed to my aunty's house, where I would be staying in Argalio. Ashur came with us to my aunty's house and didn't show much interest in his family or spending time with them.

Over time, he began to sleep over at my aunty's house, and we all became very comfortable with each other. Every day he would take me out sightseeing and show me around. My aunty would follow everywhere we went. We would walk in front, and she would follow directly behind us to make sure that I was safe and to ensure that Ashur couldn't touch me. One day when we were left alone, he decided to take me to his house.

Now that we were alone, we could finally talk. We finally were together once again in the flesh after a year apart. It felt like so much longer. "It is so good to see you again" he said to me. "I never believed that you and I would come back together again! I'm so excited to be with you."

He was no longer living with his sister by that time. The place he was living was not far from where my aunty lived. He took me back to his place and gave me a grand tour. He wanted to show me something he had drawn on the wall. I looked at the wall and saw a hand-drawn heart shape with the initials "A & I" inside it—a very romantic gesture and his way of showing me that he truly loved me and truly did want to be with me. I knew he thought about me a lot.

He slept on a mattress on the floor directly next to the wall where our initials were. I pictured him staring time and time again at the wall and picturing us together again. This filled my heart with warmth and made me feel so happy, warm, and fuzzy inside. He really was thinking about me. Was I in love?

While we were there, I was introduced to one of his friends. The coincidence was that I knew him. When I was at school, there was a boy I used to share study notes with who was my age. We went to separate schools (I was at a girl's school, and of course, he was at a boy's school). We would swap books at school when we were studying the same subjects.

I recall I used to go onto my roof and throw my books down to him. He was so lovely; he would always come and find me and make sure I had all of the correct books and study notes. He used to write me love letters and put them in my books after he found out that I was with Ashur. I never saw him as anything more than a friend. We grew up together, and I saw him as a brother figure. He had fled Iraq because he didn't want to go into the army and ended up in Greece. He had a half-sister (they shared the same father) who lived with my aunty.

This particular character tried anything and everything he possibly could to tear Ashur and I apart. He was telling lies, telling him that I was the one writing love letters, that I always wanted to be with him. I pulled him aside at once and asked him why he was so insistent on causing trouble and tension in my relationship. My aunty had spoken to him as well as his sister, all trying to convince him to stop causing trouble between Ashur and I.

Ashur ignored everything he was told because he felt that this friend was jealous. We kept our distance from him after that.

We loved living in Greece. I loved everything about the place: the history, the islands, everything. However, we couldn't work, and sometimes we could not even eat. There was no way to live or survive.

During this time, one of Ashur's sisters kissed her sister's husband (Con, who was married to Ashur's sister who already lived in Greece). Con's wife, my sister-in-law, never found out that her husband had betrayed her with her very own sister. On the positive side, it was only ever a kiss and nothing more. He felt that he was in love with her.

This was all so shameful for Ashur, and he decided to send them back to Iraq. He sent a letter to his father telling him to arrange flights for his mother and brothers and sisters to all come back. I begged him not to do this and insisted that we all get one big house and live together. If we all worked and contributed, we could survive. He refused to listen and demanded that they all go back.

His mother blamed me, thinking that I was the one who didn't want them to be around any longer. Ashur insisted that he was only looking after me, and the rest had to go back to Iraq. He gave no explanation to his father, simply said to arrange flights for them all. All he said was that he no longer wanted to be responsible for them.

Ashur's father was planning on eventually moving to Greece himself, but his oldest son was in the army in Iraq so he needed to stay and support him as well as work to send money to his children living in Greece, as they were not citizens and couldn't work in the country.

Around a month after this incident, on August 16, 1977, Ashur and I got married. On this very same day, Elvis Presley died. Elvis was my idol. I knew very well that this was not a good sign. It was bad luck and a warning to me. I didn't quite know what the warning was, but it sure was a sign trying to tell me something.

There was a fellow invited to our wedding who, not long after we had announced our engagement, had met a girl from Iraq who was a relative of mine. Her mother had been maid of honour at my mother's wedding, and thus we were all family. They continued to date happily, and soon after, he got engaged and married this girl—as if to prove to me that he was doing all of this because of me. We stood next to them at their wedding, as their *koumbari*. A great honour.

We spent a lot of time together as a group. We would go out for dinner together, have dinner parties at home, and go out as a group. We ended up becoming very close.

Ashur had sent all of his family back (except his sister who was already married in Greece), and the rumours had started that I was the one who didn't want them around. My mother-in-law began to resent me. Let's not forget, she didn't like me to begin with, and I was an easy target to direct the blame at. After all, nobody will look at themselves and point the finger of blame.

Once this drama had started, even before we were married, my aunty began to get on my case about wanting to marry Ashur. She was constantly nagging at me wanting me to throw the ring away and not make the mistake of marrying him, but I was so in love with him. We wanted to be together.

Once the family had returned to Iraq, we lived with his sister and brother-in-law for a while. During this time, I witnessed horrific physical assaults that my sister-in-law was subjected to by her husband. Perhaps he began to resent her, because he was not truly in love with her and was in fact in love with her sister. We will never know. All I know is that I could no longer simply sit back and watch him beat her until she was black and blue constantly and for no reason.

I was so young. I recall one day when we were at home, I was ironing, and he had beaten her up so badly that I intervened and threatened to smash him in the face with the hot iron. I realised very quickly that I needed to get out of that house. Shortly after, we moved in with my aunty (my father's sister).

CHAPTER 5

IT'S LIKE RIDING A BIKE

One day, one of the guys found a bicycle abandoned in the street. Found, stole, who knows? He marched straight into the house, proud as anything, ready to show off this new bike.

We couldn't leave the bike abandoned the front of our house. It was common for bicycles in those days to be stolen and dumped, as they were a cheap form of transport. However, if you were caught with a stolen bike, the Greek police were a force to be reckoned with. We were always so careful to be pleasant and law-abiding, as we were not legal citizens of the country. To avoid getting any of us into trouble, we bought the bike inside the house so it could not be seen by the police, thus avoiding any questioning or trouble.

At one stage my father's cousin came to visit from America to organise my aunty's documentation so she could go to America. He stayed with us for a week. The documentation was like a marriage certificate for American immigration. We had such a great time. We drank, partied, and laughed every day.

The first night after my cousin arrived, he was sitting going through the documentation with my aunty. Ashur approached him in a random encounter and said, "I had a dream about you. I dreamt that you had smuggled drugs into the country. They were in a cigarette packet. Do you have drugs on you?"

My cousin looked at Ashur and laughed uncontrollably. My cousin had not spoken a word about it from the airport. He had managed to get away with smuggling marijuana into the country through a sealed packet of Marlboro cigarettes—such a popular cigarette brand in those days. He stayed with us for a week, so it was not suspicious at all.

That particular night, they all smoked marijuana with my cousin. My aunty began to panic, saying, "Oh my God, they're going to catch us! We're all going to be locked up or shipped off back home!" Although she was in a panic, she was awfully curious about what the men were smoking and of course insisted on trying it.

All the men went outside, standing in the street stoned. My aunty and I were inside the house. The men were like children, taking turns riding the bike up and down the street, laughing and carrying on. As they were fooling around with the bike, an unmarked, undercover police car drove by. I was very scared and panicked because it was a stolen bike. Thank God the police did not check the bike.

CHAPTER 6

WAKE UP! IT'S A SIGN!

Greece gave me a lot of good signs—moments that made me question myself and my life, and moments of what felt like awakening. We had such a wonderful day on our wedding day. We laughed, drank, danced, and ate a lot of delicious Greek food. Then, suddenly, the day was over.

I had married the love of my life. We were together now. Nobody could tell us what to do. It was just the two of us, ready to take on the world and live happily ever after. Oh the taste of freedom and the bounce in my step when I came to realise all of this.

The night of our wedding, we went back to our hotel room, and my new husband attacked me. I didn't know what he was doing to me. He was touching me inappropriately and in ways that I had never been touched before. I panicked! I grabbed a knife and told him to get away from me. I threatened to kill him if he didn't. I ran into the bathroom, locked myself in, and wouldn't come out.

I didn't even know what happens when you get married. My perception of marriage was that you simply kiss and cuddle and hold hands. How naive I was.

My mother or aunties never discussed sex. That was embarrassing. After my experience, I spoke to my aunty, who explained to me all the details of how sexual intercourse happens. A little too late, if you ask me. They could have saved me the shame and told me a little sooner.

After being married for six months, we went to live with my aunty. A month or two later, I was pregnant. The aunty we lived with was a heavy drinker. She had lost her husband tragically; he had drowned under mysterious circumstances, and the matter was never delved into. She needed to leave Iraq and so moved to Greece. My father sent me to Greece to be close to her. Once I fell pregnant, she started to turn nasty towards me. All of her life she had wanted children but could not bear them. She began to show signs of jealousy towards me.

While we were living in Greece, the Assyrian community had bound together and would have functions and events. This kept us occupied and put a positive spin on a bitter, difficult life for us. One day while I was around two months pregnant, we went on a day trip—two busloads of us—and went to a very beautiful place. It was like paradise. It had a natural spring-water waterfall and a church of St. John.

According to the stories told, St. John was burnt by the Turks, and his body was mummified and buried in a glass tomb within this church. The church was a beautiful old church, full of nuns and monks. You could walk all around the glass tomb, and you could see him mummified. On one side of his face, you could see his teeth. The other side was all gold.

I always have felt connected to the church, to God, and to my spiritual side. There was a nun who came to us and said, "If you believe, take a stone outside the church, pray, make your wish, and place it on the side of the church. If it sticks, your prayers will be answered." Some people's stones stuck, but many didn't. I held my stone and prayed so hard. I prayed for a healthy baby boy, to get out of Greece, and to start a better life. When I realised that my stone had stuck, I yelped, "It's stuck!"

The nun came over to me and said, "You are a very strong believer, and God will answer your wishes."

It felt as though the whole ground of the church was alive—a light that was pulling me towards it. As we were leaving, one of the buses got stuck there and could not move. The occupants of that bus had to stay the night. The monks gave up their rooms, and the patrons stayed in those rooms.

I looked at my husband and said, "Why couldn't our bus stop? I wanted to stay. It was so beautiful there."

This place was like paradise. The water was cold, crisp, and clear, even in the heat of summer. All the trees and fruit were green and lush, and the water was so fresh. If there was anywhere in the world I would love to live, it would be at that very place. I still have a photo of this place. It was so picturesque and magical.

During my pregnancy, I began to have some bizarre dreams. This is when I had my first awakening. I had a dream that I was back in Iraq in the old house where we used to live. It was very dark. Through the darkness, I could see the silhouette of Jesus. He came to me, sat calmly by my bedside, and said to me, "Take your husband and leave this house."

I approached my husband and spoke to him about my dream and the message that was given to me. He was very quick to dismiss it because he was used to me telling him about my dreams all the time. In the meantime, my aunty became quite violent. She had become resentful towards me and physically abusive. She would beat me regularly, and this was becoming more frequent.

A second dream occurred. I saw the silhouette of Jesus Christ again, and this time he was very upset with me. He was very disappointed and wondering why I wasn't listening to him. He said to me, "What are you doing? I told you to leave!"

This was concerning. I spoke to my husband again and told him this must be a sign, and we needed to leave. Again, and as usual, he dismissed what I was saying. I was trying to shut out the dreams and ignore them in hopes that this was pure coincidence and that I perhaps was overanalysing everything. Meanwhile, I was becoming more heavily pregnant and being subjected to more frequent physical abuse from my aunty.

A third dream came about where again I saw the same silhouette of Jesus who came to me. This time he was angry. He was aggressive and determined to make his point. He looked at me and in a very dismissive voice said, "What did I tell you? I told you to leave. If you don't leave, I will break this house over your head."

This time, I told my husband that if he didn't want to leave, I was going on my own. I knew that this was a sign and that I needed to protect myself and my baby. The sign was telling me that something was going to harm me and my baby.

I went to stay with my *koumbari*. I stayed on the floor there, and my husband finally followed me. We decided, the four of us, to move and get a house all together. We found a house, furnished it, and moved in. At this stage, I was seven months pregnant.

Here we had great memories. We had lovely neighbours who would bring me food for the baby—guardian angels protecting me. God had sent me to a better place. Music would play, and there was fun, laughter, and plenty of joy around me. We would eat, drink, be merry, and have a good time.

My sister-in-law's husband was a great big strong man. They would come and visit and help with whatever they could. We were illegal immigrants and were unable to work. We would ration our food.

There was a curtain that separated the bedroom from the rest of the house. In my seventh month of pregnancy, I was in bed and awkwardly trying to make myself comfortable. My husband was snoring fast asleep next to me. It was like I was in a trance as I saw the door opening. I was frozen; I couldn't move or scream. I saw this person open the curtains and come through. I couldn't see if it was someone I knew.

I could see in his eyes, sun, brightness, long hair. He looked like a shepherd. He was talking to me telepathically. He was asking me if I was okay and telling me that he had brought all of these things to me and wanted to make sure I was okay. Throughout this conversation, I was telling him that I was scared. He was comforting me and telling me that I would be okay and not to worry. I felt pinned to the bed as if I had been paralysed. I could not move at all.

I told him, "I want a boy."

He turned to me, smiled, and in a soft confiding voice said, "I know what you want. You don't need to tell me." He stood up, turned his back, opened the curtain, walked out, and closed the door.

I finally could move. I got up and screamed. Everybody woke up. I told them Jesus was here. Nobody believed me. I told them, "You will all see. This house will be blessed. I am going to be blessed with a boy, and my son will be blessed. We are going to go somewhere."

Two months after I had these dreams, I gave birth to my healthy baby boy. At the time, I was just a young girl. Nobody told me anything or explained to me how you have babies or what would happen to me or my body. I ended up in the public hospital system in Greece, which felt like the worst hospital in the world.

I recall somebody touching and poking my stomach and asking if it felt okay. I kept asking where my baby was. All I remember is waking up the next day out of it and asking for my baby. I stayed in the hospital for only a couple of days, but it was one of the worst experiences of my life. It was dirty. I just wanted to get out of there.

I began to look for my way out of Greece, to get out and start a fresh life. All doors were closed to Australia, America, Canada … Once we realised how difficult it was to get out, we quickly came to realise that we had to do something in Greece to better our lives.

ILLEGAL IMMIGRANTS

In Greece, we couldn't work as illegal immigrants. Whoever worked would do so illegally, and the pay was not good. This made life an even bigger struggle.

Paint a picture of protest, hardship, difficulty. We Assyrians all gathered, and there was a community meeting of about six hundred people. We gathered and sat on the floor of the United Nations representative as a protest. One of the representatives came out and asked what was going on.

A leader stood up and spoke on behalf of all refugees living in Greece from Iraq. He asked what they were going to do to help the situation. The authorities said there was nothing they could do. They threatened us and told us that if we refused to leave, they would drag us out of there. The police came and took all of the men and put them in jail. My *koumbari* also went to jail because she refused to leave her husband's side. During this time, the men were interrogated and questioned as to why they were doing what they were doing—why they were protesting.

My husband spoke to the head of the police and explained the situation. This man knew the story already. My husband and the others were told that they would be released but that there was nothing that could be done. The men linked arms and refused to leave. One of the police representatives told my husband that he had a baby and that he was better off leaving. Our men refused to leave, and the police got violent and started to scare them.

The United Nations became involved and released the men. I was so scared at the time. I was alone with my baby and had no phone for contact.

The men were promised that they would be given a head office to deal with their political refugee issues to make contact with Australia, Canada, and America to see where they could go. We had tried to go to America, but our application had been rejected. At that stage, I had no passport; my passport had expired. The United Nations granted me political refugee status and granted me a passport for myself, my husband, and my son.

A church counsel who worked with the United Nations funded us to come to Australia, which had just opened its doors for refugees. My son was around six months old when we were finally granted access into Australia. We were interviewed, questioned, and asked why we wanted to come to Australia. We discussed the poor treatment of Assyrians in Iraq and how poorly treated we were.

During this time, the Assyrian community stuck together. We were a very family-oriented people, peaceful, harmonious, and never making trouble. We all bound together within the community and would share food, money, etc.

A lot of Assyrian women worked illegally in factories, and some were unfortunate enough to have lost fingers, hands, and limbs in these factories and these jobs. Children were starving.

We were lucky that my husband's family sent us some money, for we had very little money to eat. Others were not so lucky. Life in Greece was very difficult, but we had a good time too. The Greek people were so hospitable; they had large, warm hearts. They would bring me food when I was pregnant and say, "Gia to pedi, fae fae!" which meant "For the baby, eat, eat!"

Fortunately, we had the courage to stick up for ourselves and protest for what we needed. That silent protest raised awareness and brought to the Greek government's attention that this was a genuine issue that had to be dealt with and fast. Naturally, the government wanted its reputation and hands cleaned of the matter, so they made arrangements as swiftly as possible to help our community. I didn't feel like I was in a strange country, but I knew I had to leave.

I recall when I first moved to Greece, I cried nonstop for a week. I had left my father behind and my sisters. But I had to leave Iraq.

Eventually, our *koumbari* left Greece bound for America in search of a better life. My aim was to get to America also, because a lot of my family was there. However, since our applications were denied, I had to look at where would be best to raise my child, and Australia was a place for me to call home.

MOVING TO AUSTRALIA

Once we arrived in Melbourne, the Council of Churches looked after us. They were connected and worked closely with the United Nations. They put us up in a hotel room for the night. They even provided a house for us to live in. The organisation had fully furnished our house down to every small detail, including cutlery. They had found my husband a job working for Ford, one of the largest motor vehicle manufacturers in the country.

A tutor was sent to my house free of charge to teach me to speak English. However, I did not have her tutor me for very long, as the English she was teaching me were basic words I already knew. I needed to learn to speak the language on a day-to-day basis. Simply learning how to say *door* and *chair* was trivial for me. I was already educated enough for this.

Once I stopped having tutoring sessions, I began to teach myself English by watching television and movies, understanding conversations, and learning words and the language through the magic of television.

Three months after we had been living in Australia and adjusting to life in an English-speaking country—trying to raise a baby, learn a foreign language, and settle into our new life in Melbourne—my husband started to change. I noticed that he was behaving differently. Something was not quite right, and I was not sure what was going on. He began to go out on his own with new friends that he'd made. He went to nightclubs and didn't come home until the early hours of the morning.

During this time, he had met a woman who worked in a bar as a bartender. She had a great reputation for not being very self-respectful, and in fact she was known in the Assyrian community for her reputation of having slept with almost the entire male Assyrian population in Melbourne. The bar she worked at attracted a lot of the Assyrian community as a meeting point, hence her reputation.

I began to worry and wonder why Ashur would come home so late. There were times when he would come home at three or four in the morning without explanation. When I began to question him on his whereabouts, he would argue with me and ask me why I wanted to know everything and tell me that nothing was going on; he was "just out."

One night, he didn't come home at all. I was so worried and stressed. I got dressed, left my baby at home, went upstairs to where another Assyrian couple lived, and asked for the husband's help. He knew something that I didn't, and I pleaded for his help with this situation. I knew that Ashur had made a new friend, Sam, who he was out with all of the time. I asked this man who Sam was in hopes that this stranger might be able to help me find my husband. The man couldn't help me any further.

I was in a huge panic, wondering whether something had happened to my husband. Every strange and deluded thought went through my mind. Had he been kidnapped? Perhaps the strange behaviour was because he was being threatened by somebody. Had he become involved with the wrong crowd? Jesus! Had the Mafia got him? Had he been killed? Drugged? I had to find answers. I needed to find my husband and make sure he was safe.

I went looking through Ashur's clothes for some unknown reason and strangely enough came across a piece of paper with an address on it in his suit jacket breast pocket. I went to the local milk bar (convenience store) down the road from my house and asked the store owner if he could tell me where this address was.

The man said to me, "This is in Pascoe Vale; it's not very far from here at all. Take a taxi, and you will be there in less than ten minutes."

I had to go to this address in the hope that I would get the answers I was looking for. I didn't know exactly what I was looking for, I just needed to make sure nothing had happened to my husband. The longer he was missing, the more I found myself imagining strange and mysterious "what if" circumstances in my head.

I spoke to my neighbour, who couldn't help me with any information, and told him that I had found this address and that it was nearby, so I was going to go and see whether anybody knew anything and what my husband's connection to this address was. He insisted that I shouldn't go by myself and that he would come with me. So with my baby asleep at home on his own, we went off in search of this address.

We arrived at the address, and it was a housing commission block of flats. I went to the door with my neighbour and knocked. A lady answered; I asked her if this was the correct address and whether she knew anybody called Ashur. She happened to be Lebanese and spoke Arabic, so we spoke more comfortably in that language.

This woman said she had never heard of Ashur, so what was this address doing in my husband's jacket pocket? I walked away feeling so empty. I had gotten nowhere. This was the only lead I had to get closer to finding my husband. My neighbour in the meantime had stayed at the door and continued speaking with her. I was telling him to hurry up and that we should leave—we had the wrong address.

My neighbour had warned the woman that she better not be hiding this man, because I was his wife and would figure out what was going on, and I would be back. I was already downstairs, but my neighbour called out to me to come back. I was stubborn and didn't see any reason to go back upstairs, since it was a dead-end lead and I was back to where I started. I didn't have the time or energy to waste, so I asked why I needed to go back upstairs.

My neighbour turned to me and said, "Come upstairs, he is here. Your husband is inside."

Shaking, in shock, and furious because this woman lied to me and I couldn't understand why, I stormed up the stairs back to her door. Why would a strange woman who doesn't even know me lie to me like that? What reason would she have to hide something like that from me when she could clearly see how frazzled I was about my missing husband? That bitch! By this stage, my sense of worry and panic had turned to pure rage and anger.

I asked where he was, and I got no answer. I stormed through the door. The woman's daughter was standing in the room, and she pointed to the wardrobe through the bedroom door and said to me, "In the cupboard."

With blood rushing through my veins and what felt like my heart pumping through my chest, I swung the cupboard door open and there he was, my husband, naked in this woman's wardrobe! Hiding from me. They were committing adultery in this strange woman's house with her young daughter nearby.

So this began to explain his strange behaviour. This was where he had been until all hours of the morning. I demanded that he tell me what was going on, and all he could say was that she was "nobody." In which way is it normal for a nobody to have somebody's husband naked in a closet and insist nothing is going on?

I stormed out of the room and grabbed this woman and threatened to kill her. I had her by the throat, and in my raging fury I began to scream at her: "Do you know he's married and has a child? That's my husband! Our baby is at home!"

She proclaimed her innocence and insisted that she didn't know that he was married and said that he had lied to her. I looked her and said, "Well, now that you know, what are you going to do about it?"

She turned to me and calmly replied, "Well, it's up to him what he would like to do."

That was enough to set alarm bells off in my head. I began to call her every foul name imaginable. What a bitch! That slut! She was breaking up my family. Destroying it! What was worse was her blasé attitude. She didn't show any remorse or any sign that she even cared in the slightest.

I grabbed a chair and swung it at her to hit her, but my husband and my neighbour stopped me and held me back. I turned to my husband and said, "Are you coming or what?" He followed with his tail between his legs.

I demanded that he give me a full explanation. Where did he meet her? Why was he doing this to me? He told me he met her in a bar that she worked in.

Foolishly, I thought through the situation and realised that I still loved this man. He was the father of my child, my husband, and I should forgive him. Having accepted this, I let the situation be, and I chose to forgive and forget. I asked him whether he was going to do this to me again, and he proclaimed his love for me, told me how remorseful and sorry he was, and swore that he would not do this again.

A month or two later, I noticed a similar pattern of behaviour—late nights, no phone calls, no explanations. Sure enough, he was going back to her. My newest occupation had become going to her address, finding my husband, spitting on this woman, and bringing him back home. I spent a very long time going back and forth between leaving my baby alone at home to go and find my cheating husband and dragging his sorry existence back home to his family. This went on for months.

One day, he came home and told me she was pregnant. It turned out she was in fact lying about the pregnancy; however, he believed her and said that he couldn't let her go because she was pregnant.

On another occasion, he went out and bought a car—a brand-new sporty two-door coupe Ford Cortina. He financed the car under my name without my permission. I asked how he could afford this car. This woman had taught him all of the shifty tricks of how to get a car through finance and go about doing dodgy things.

This woman was thirty-seven years old, married and divorced with a child, and my husband was nineteen years old at the time. She had one leg shorter than the other and was nothing special to look at. Taking all of this into consideration, my husband could still not keep away from her. It was as though she had cast a spell on him, like black magic.

Once the Assyrian community began to hear about my situation and that we were married and had a child and my husband was committing adultery with this slut of a woman, they bound together and wanted to do something about it. The young men made a plot to beat him up and teach him a lesson. One night he went out to the club and these men beat the daylights out of him. He came home black and blue.

Ashur had family who lived in Sydney, and his uncle came to Melbourne to visit, assess our situation, and see whether there was something he could do to help. He came to our house, and I told him that Ashur was not home and the only place to find my husband was at this woman's house. I told him that if he didn't believe me, I would take him there right away.

We went together straight to this woman's house—and sure enough, there was my husband with black and blue eyes, bruised and sore, in this woman's house. His uncle asked him what happened, and Ashur told us they had bashed him to his core. I told him that they should have killed him.

The men who beat him were so disgusted with him. They were yelling at him and spitting on him and telling him he should be ashamed of himself. My husband thought that I had plotted for this to happen, but little did he know that I had no idea. I had not even spoken to anybody about it. It was simply the fact that they believed that he was doing the wrong thing and wanted to do something about it.

I did not even know the men who had done this to him. I knew one of them whose name was also Ashur. I had met him one time at our house when he came to visit. He was dating this woman at one stage; she wouldn't leave him alone and he threatened to kill her if she didn't leave him alone. As soon as this man heard what she was doing with Ashur, he spoke to his friends and they made a plot to teach my husband a lesson.

I just didn't know what to do anymore. I had nobody to talk to, nobody to turn to or confide in. It seemed that I was last to know everything. Everybody knew what was going on well before I did. I prayed to God, Jesus, and Mary for their help every night. I was desperate. I was helpless. What should I do? I needed help from a higher power.

One night my husband came home and snuck into the house. He slowly and quietly took off his jacket so as not to wake me. As he walked into our bedroom where I was sleeping, he saw the silhouette of a dark woman standing in the doorway of the bedroom. She looked evil; her eyes beamed on him like lasers. She had a sure grin on her face and shook her index finger side to side at him. She blocked the entrance into the room and leant with one hand up against the door frame as if to tell him that no, he was not allowed into the room.

The coincidence was that only days earlier, I'd had a dream of this silhouette of a dark woman who looked terribly evil coming to attack me. Somebody stood between us and protected me. When Ashur described the woman to me, it seemed to be the silhouette of the same woman, but in his vision, she was protecting me.

This frightened the life out of my husband, and he crawled into bed with me and held me all night. He was so scared and so spooked that he couldn't stop thinking about it and couldn't sleep. We spoke about what he saw, and I told him that this was probably a sign. Somebody was trying to teach him a lesson or send him a message to warn him as punishment for what he was doing to me. I told him that somebody would most likely stop him from what he was doing, and probably not in a very nice manner.

I told him that I couldn't handle living this life anymore. Some drastic changes had to be made to our lifestyle if our relationship, marriage, and family had any hope of surviving. I suggested we move to Sydney to try to build a new life there. This way, we would be as far away from this woman as possible, and we'd have my husband's family members there also so we would not be alone.

He agreed that this was a good idea, and I began plans to move. I sold everything I had and was ready to go. Ashur sold his car, kept all the money, and didn't pay off the finance—all this without my knowledge. I ended up with a bad credit rating because my husband had pulled some shifty moves.

I left for Sydney with my son first, and he was going to follow a few days later. As soon as I arrived in Sydney I went out in search of a job. Very soon I had found myself a job working for a fly-screen company. My job was to install all of the screens onto the frames, which I enjoyed. My work environment was positive, it was relaxed, and I was earning money to survive and make a living.

I was staying with Ashur's relatives until I could save some money to find a place with my husband and son to live together. But Ashur never came to Sydney. His uncle, aunty, cousins, and all of his relatives were calling him to find out where he was and what was going on, and they could not get in contact with him. After a couple of months of unsuccessful attempts, I realised that he was not coming. I could no longer rely on these people to keep a roof over my head. It was time to find my own home and move out.

Not long after, I began to sift through a real estate agent's listings, and I found myself and my son a little flat to live in. It was a small two-bedroom flat in Fairfield. I had no furniture. The only things I had were my son's cot and blankets. I slept on the floor for three months. Every so often, I would go to second-hand sales and auctions and buy bits and pieces along the way. Whoever came to visit sat on the floor.

On the bright side, at least I knew that the people who were coming to visit me were coming for me, and they didn't care whether they were sitting on the floor or not. I also bought myself an old second-hand black-and-white television. Over time, I bought a bed and other pieces of furniture.

Eventually, Ashur turned up. He became fed up with everybody questioning him and telling him off about the situation he had caused. Everybody who knew me knew very well that I was a very decent person and kind-hearted, and I had a good reputation in the community.

Throughout this whole process, the lifestyle I was subjected to had caused so much stress that I had lost an abundance of weight. I had become anaemic and almost anorexic. I wasn't eating; the mere thought of food was not anywhere near my mind. As long as my son was healthy and he was fed, that's all that mattered to me. I couldn't eat or sleep. I was stressed, and it was constant.

I went to the doctor in desperate need of help. I was begging him to prescribe sleeping pills for me so I could at least rest. The doctor refused to give me sleeping pills and told me that if I didn't act fast, I would either die or end up in a mental institution. I was depressed, and I was financially broken. I was now unemployed and desperate. I'd had to leave my job, as it was too far away from where I was living and I had no means to get to and from work.

My *koumbari* who was my maid of honour when I got married in Greece was living in Sydney. Her husband owned his own bank branch there and was quite well known in the community as a prosperous businessman. This man knew a lot about the legal system and the Australian government. Once he saw how desperate I was—young, alone, a single mother, and unemployed in an unfamiliar city in a foreign country—helping me became a matter of urgency for him. He explained to me that given my situation, the government would be able to offer me some financial assistance. I had no idea what he was talking about.

He made appointments for me at the social security office, and soon after I started receiving a small amount of money from them, which helped me with my rent. In the meantime, I found myself a part-time job and was able to make some money and buy more furniture. I went into a store with a good friend of mine that help me to as a guarantor so that's how they give me the credit and arranged for finance and had my home fully furnished. New television! How exciting! Although my life was a struggle in many ways, I was lucky enough and blessed to have the support of the Assyrian community in Sydney.

Occasionally, I would have a surprise visit from Ashur. Each time he came to Sydney, he stayed with me and our son. He would stay for a week and then do the Houdini and vanish. What I wasn't aware of (this became news to me later in life) was that every time he would come to Sydney from Melbourne, his Lebanese girlfriend was with him. He would hide her from me, leave her somewhere, and come and stay with me.

During this time while he was coming to visit, I fell pregnant. There I was, a single mother with an on-again off-again runaway husband, just getting my life on track, and pregnant again. I was lost, confused, and not sure what I should do. Once I found out that I was pregnant, I contacted him, trying to let him know that we were having another baby. When I finally got hold of him, his reaction was dull, dismissive, and to the point. He told me he didn't care, and I could do whatever I wanted to with my child. He had no interest in being a father.

ABORTION

At three months pregnant, I couldn't handle all of the pressure in my life. How was I going to raise two children on my own? How would I look after them? I found myself having to make the most painful decision of my life and abort my unborn child. My *koumbari* came with me along with another friend of mine to support me.

At this time, abortion was a dangerous procedure to have done. I was devastated when I found out that I had just let go of my unborn little baby girl. As soon as Ashur's relatives found out that this is what had occurred, they went on a manhunt. They were determined that they were going to kill him. I pleaded with them to leave him alone, as there was no point even trying to reason with this man any longer.

I went to visit my local priest, who by this stage knew me well. He helped me and was willing to assist with the filing of divorce papers. Usually, divorce was not allowed unless both parties agreed or there had been a substantial time of separation. The priest knew my situation, however, and agreed to assist with lodgement for divorce, as he was fully aware that my husband was committing adultery and was not committed to our marriage. He knew there were many people in the community who could testify and be proof of that. At this stage, I had been living in Sydney for two and a half years.

In the meantime, Ashur spoke to the local priest in Melbourne and said that I had forced him to go to Sydney, and that it was not his choice. He never really wanted to go there, but if I returned to Melbourne, we could work on our marriage and relationship. I thought about it, I pondered, and I chose to forgive him. I made the choice not to break up my family because of his behaviour.

ATTEMPTED SUICIDE

I was at the breaking point. On one occasion, I even attempted suicide. If he hadn't closed the car door, I would've died. I was only eighteen or nineteen years old at this stage. This whole ordeal had occurred over two or three years.

When I agreed to go back to Melbourne and give our family one last chance at being together, I packed all of my furniture and arranged for a removalist to send all of my belongings to Melbourne. Once I was packed and organised, I moved out of my home in Sydney and came back to Melbourne. I had told Ashur to arrange a place for us to live so that when I came back, the move would be easier. Upon my arrival back in Melbourne, however, I found that there was no home. I had paid over $1,000 to have the removalist truck bring all my belongings to Melbourne. In the eighties, $1,000 was like $10,000, especially for a single mother working part-time.

A friend of mine from Greece who was living in Melbourne agreed to help me and kept all of my furniture in storage in her garage for me. I also stayed with her for a few months until I could find a new place. I searched and searched for the right place and finally find myself a home. It took quite some time to move and settle in again. It felt as though since being in this country, I had done nothing but pack and move with my son.

Once I was settled in, Houdini made an appearance and moved in. This time, I found out that he was no longer with the previous woman who I had met. He was with another woman, and this woman in fact had fallen pregnant and had a baby with my husband. Had I known this before moving back to Melbourne, I would've stayed in Sydney and never returned to Melbourne. It was too late now for could-have-been and should-have-been.

One of Ashur's friends had come to me to inform me that he had a child with this woman, and if I didn't believe it, then I should ask Ashur myself. The shame came from the fact that everybody in the community knew what was going on except me. My husband was sleeping around, going from woman to woman. I'd married a male whore.

This particular lady had been living in Melbourne and was from New Zealand. After being with him in an on-again, off-again relationship for three months, she fell pregnant with his child. He had told her that he already had one child and did not want to have any more. For this reason, this woman chose not to tell him that she was pregnant. It was too dangerous for her to abort her child; there was some sort of complication or disorder with her blood, and the health risks and complications were enormous.

Because they were on-again off-again, he'd had no idea that she was even pregnant. Once she had given birth to her child, she told him they had a son. Ashur was not even remotely interested in knowing that this child even existed. He told her that this was her child and she could do whatever she pleased. He made it clear that he wanted nothing to do with it. Once he found out that she was the mother of his new son, he made his signature Houdini move.

I questioned my husband and wanted to know whether this story were true. He admitted to having this child and produced a photo from his wallet of this baby. His son looked identical to our son as a baby. There was no denying this was in fact his child. Once I saw this photo and had confirmation of this story being true, I turned to him calmly, told him to grab his belongings, told him he was a fucking idiot, and demanded that he leave and never return again. I told him that he had destroyed any love that I had in my heart for him. He had stabbed me right in the middle of the heart that contained unconditional and undying love for him.

I told him it was over, and "I never want to see you or hear from you again." Ten years after I married the love of my life, I finally got my divorce.

While I was separated, my brother-in-law came to live with me. He had come to Australia, and Ashur had not given him the time of day, so I had him come and stay with me. It worked well. He helped me raise my son, and once my son started school, he would take my son to and from school. It allowed me to go and work as a cleaner. He would help with looking after my son and was a wonderful father figure.

After a while, the rumours started about there being something going on between my brother-in-law and me. My brother-in-law came to me and told me that I was such a lovely person and I had done so much for him; not even his own brother looked after him or ever did for him what I had done. However, it was time for him to move out, because he did not want to cause any heartache for me or escalate any rumours. I was left on my own again, working two different jobs to survive, trying to raise my son.

In the meantime, Ashur had found himself a new woman. This one was more stable and secure, which was better for him. She was fifteen years older than him. He loved his older women.

At this point, I was starting to make so much sense of what had happened in my life. My husband used to have coffee late at night with my brother-in-law's brother's wife. Her husband was never there. We always assumed that they were just good friends but later came to realise what late-night coffees really meant. This man had been cheating on me from day one. I was simply a naive toy for him in his sick little game of life. On the grand scale of things, I was nothing to him. This is the person that he was.

The man I had fallen head over heels and truly, madly, deeply in love with was a lying, cheating fool who used women as objects and dragged me over hot coals, through hell and back, so many times with no mercy before simply walking away. I was blinded by my love for him, and now I had a child with him. I was not able to just walk away.

I didn't know many people in Melbourne, just a few friends. I did have some relatives who lived there, and once I came back to live in Melbourne, I began to spend a lot more time with this one particular family. The father was a distant uncle of mine, and he had eight daughters and a son. This family looked after me like I was their daughter and sister. They told me I wasn't the one who had done anything wrong and that I had their full support. My aunty was married to the father's brother. It was my aunty's brother-in-law.

The girls loved me. We all got along very well. We would sit around for hours and chat, read coffee cups, laugh, and enjoy each other's company. This was a very difficult time for me trying to deal with what was happening to me. I was not interested in looking at any men. I was so young and had men chasing me around, but I never gave anybody a chance. I was still in love with Ashur. Once I found out he had another child, my heart broke.

COSTA

I met many men after this. One of them was Costa, a man I became engaged to marry. That's another story from hell.

We met in a club. We were interested in each other. Although I was young and attracting a lot of attention from men, for some reason I was attracted to this one. He lived in Richmond—a Greek man. He told me he would do anything for me.

The problem was that he was a heavy gambler. Not only was he a heavy gambler; he was involved with bookies and was gambling big money. We were engaged and living together in Richmond. He was gambling big with horses and bookies. I was living life at the edge of my seat. Always on edge, worried about how dangerous the scene he was involved in was. I had my young son and was so worried and pleaded with him time and time again to stop his gambling.

SHAMIRAM

My distant cousin Shamiram came to live with me. Well, she was not a cousin, but she was related to me somehow. She was a young girl who had married when she was fourteen years old and had a baby. She was around fifteen or sixteen when I met her again in Australia.

She had grown up in the north of Iraq, as country folk. They lived a very simple life and lived off the land. She was illiterate and had never been to school; she had no education or social skills. She slept next to sheep in stables.

She married a relative of my aunty's husband. After she got married, she fell pregnant, and while she was pregnant, they travelled through the countryside of Iraq by foot for days and weeks into Iran. They trekked through the mountains, as in those days it was very difficult to leave the country. They lived in Iran until the late 1980s, when they left Iran as refugees. Her husband's brother lived in Australia and helped with their documentation to have them move to Australia as political refugees.

Shamiram had her baby while they were living in Iran. They moved to Australia, and she was a housewife. Her husband was an older man, around thirty years old, although she was only fourteen when they married. This was normal in Iraq. He found himself in a position where he became a father figure to her. He had to teach her home economics from scratch. He taught her how to shower and wash herself properly, how to wash clothes, how to go to the bathroom. He even played a bigger role in raising their child than fathers usually did. He loved his child so much.

She had a brother-in-law who was single and was a dirty, sleazy, no-good son of a bitch. I knew him because I knew the whole family from Iraq. Nothing had ever changed. One of his brothers was in love with me back in Iraq. I was never interested in him.

At this stage, I was living in a housing commission flat. While they were living here, her brother-in-law was living with them. The older brother was living with his wife and children in one unit, and they were in a separate room and lived with this sleazy younger brother close by in another unit. This man had never worked a day in his life.

One time, her husband went to Sydney for a weekend, and while he was away, this brother went and tied her up, put a knife to her throat, and raped her. He untied her and told her that if she ever told anyone, he'd kill her. She didn't tell a soul. Somehow, the sister-in-law (who was married to the older brother) found out what had happened. I don't know how she found out—perhaps he went and bragged about it somewhere. She went to her husband and told him, and her husband wanted to kill his brother. They had to hide him so nobody could get to him.

As soon as Shamiram's husband found out what had happened, he threw his wife out onto the street. She was now used property and had given herself to somebody else in his eyes, regardless of whether it was against her will or not. He felt betrayed because she never told him. She explained how scared she was that the brother would kill her as he had threatened, and that's why she never said anything.

Shamiram was spaced out. She did not understand what anybody was saying to her. She was very slow to process her thoughts. She was easily confused. The local priest took her under his wing once he found out about her situation. A young girl, married, raped by her brother-in-law, and thrown out onto the streets, now homeless and away from her child. He took her into his home, and she lived with the priest and his wife.

Shamiram never knew how to read Assyrian or Arabic. She was totally illiterate. She would go to church, but she didn't actually know why. She couldn't comprehend why she was going to church. The wife of the priest after some time became jealous and couldn't stand Shamiram living there anymore. The priest and his wife had four children, and she was jealous of this other woman being in their home.

I was very involved in the Assyrian community at this time. I was involved in organising events and was quite well known within the community. The priest knew me well, he had a lot of respect for me, and he was well aware of my situation and what had happened in my life. He approached me one day to discuss the situation that this girl was in and ask for my help. He knew that she was somehow related to me, and he needed me to assist him with her situation. He said I was probably the only person who could help.

I knew she was not very intelligent, and I discussed the situation with him. He told me that he could no longer have her in his home and that his wife was a little jealous of her. I told him that she was welcome to come and stay with me, but I did not have a room for her. I had a two-bedroom flat with one room for me and one for my son. She could get a mattress and sleep on the floor in the living room. I would help her, but I would not give up my or my son's room. She had no money and no job, as she had been a housewife and was now without her son.

Shamiram came to stay with me. Every day she cried for her son. Her husband wouldn't allow her to see their child. I tried to talk to her to find out what had happened, but it was like trying to get blood out of a stone. She was unresponsive. It was so frustrating. I wanted to shake some sense into her to get her to talk to me. I tried for such a long time, but still I got nothing from her. Eventually I became so frustrated that I gave her an ultimatum and told her that if she didn't talk to me, I would throw her out.

I asked her if she had provoked her brother-in-law; all she said was no. In the end, I had to use my imagination and guess what might have happened. As I asked her questions, she would answer, until I got the full story out of her. I'd ask, "Did he do this—did he do that? Was it like this?" And she would say yes or no until all the pieces of the puzzle came together, and I discovered what her brother-in-law had done to her.

Eventually, her husband found out that she was living with me, and I spoke to him. I told him he was an asshole and asked him why he wouldn't allow her to see her son. I got very angry at him and told him that he had no right to stop her from seeing her son. I threatened to help her take him to court and gain custody of her son, and I told him that I was now her voice and would stand up for her.

He knew not to mess with me. He mellowed out slightly, and because he highly respected me, he said to me, "Ishtar, it's fine. So long as she is living with you, she can see our son." I brought her son to stay with us and now found myself in a situation where I was looking after Shamiram, her son, my son, and myself.

While they were living with me, we spent a lot of time talking and got to know each other quite well. I asked her if she understood the meaning of her religion and if she understood the symbolism of going to church. I began to ask her questions, asking her why she went to church. She had no idea. All she knew was that she had to go to church. She didn't understand any of it.

This is when I decided to take a Bible and start reading it to her. I would read passages from the Bible to her and explain what they meant and slowly started to read prayers and have her understand what her beliefs were and where they stemmed from. I explained all the prayers and their meaning. She was like a lost sheep, simply going to church because that's what everybody else did. She was a lost soul. I helped over time to bring her soul back to God.

Shamiram had a tattoo on her hand. It was similar to a cross. The cross had an eye in it, and over time the eye was growing. I asked her what it was. She looked at me dazed and said, "I don't know. Somebody did this on me." I knew this was not a good thing. I told her something was not right about it. I insisted that she have it removed. Some strange feeling had come over me, and I just knew it was bad.

She began to have problems with her skin. I asked her if she knew how to wash herself. I asked how she washed her skin and made sure she was looking after herself. She was so itchy and she had scratched the skin on her stomach so much that it had thinned out and was raw. I took her to doctors and had them run tests. They recommended topical creams for her, but they didn't help much. I knew there was more to this than met the eye.

At this stage I had met Costa, who I ended up becoming engaged to. I took her and her son with me, and they lived with us for a while until it was time for her to find her own place to live and fend for herself and her son. I wanted her to learn to be independent.

I found her a place to live in Richmond, so she was at least close to me. It was a one-bedroom flat. We put down a deposit and helped her get set up. Once she moved in, I found her a job washing dishes in a local restaurant, so she was becoming independent. She enjoyed her job there. I also worked in this restaurant part-time.

I told her that she had to fast for three days. I have no idea why, but for some reason I had to tell her to do these things. I felt that she might get a message from a higher power if she fasted for three days. She followed my instructions. Not even a drop of water entered her body. I asked her if she was hungry, and she said no.

After this fasting period, her face started to glow. She looked fresh. Something was changing in her. I knew a miracle was happening to her. I insisted that she remove the tattoo from her body. I told her to go to the hospital and have it removed with a laser. Usually there was a long waiting list for a procedure like laser tattoo removal, but by a miracle, she had an appointment within a week. It was as if somebody was looking down on her and knew she had to have this done.

She had her procedure done and was very sore. Her wrist was a weeping wound, bandaged up and excruciating. They had scrubbed out the tattoo from the skin. While she was still sore and bandaged up, Shamiram began to have some symbolic dreams. She never used to dream but was now starting to have these dreams every day. She turned to me one day and said, "Ishtar, she came to me. It was a lady. She was very tall, beautiful, and wearing long caped white clothing. She knocked on my door, and she had a blue book in her hands like the book that you used to read to me from." The Bible that I had and used to read to Shamiram had a blue cover.

She didn't know who this lady was, she just assumed it was a lady teaching her how the Bible works in her dreams. She said that the lady was teaching her about the Bible exactly like I used to. One day she came to me and said that in her dream, there was a baby in a basinet. This baby was such a gorgeous baby. The tall lady turned to Shamiram and said, "You see this baby? This is Ishtar's son." I was confused. I had no idea what this meant. I was with Costa; I already had my son.

Costa was a difficult, needy person who needed to hear that I loved him every day. One day he hit me. That was enough for me to say I was leaving. I couldn't stay with somebody who hit me. In the meantime, Mary was coming to Shamiram in her dreams and giving her the message that I needed to leave.

I had no furniture and nowhere to go. I had lost my housing commission flat because I had moved in with Costa. I told myself that I would pack, get passports ready, and leave for America. I had bought brand-new suitcases and had enough money saved to leave. I was ready to go. At this stage, my son was seven or eight years old. As I was preparing to leave, Shamiram would talk to me about these dreams she was having. She was now having dreams every day.

I used to take her to a special church in Nicholson Street with me all the time. I taught her how to pray. We would wear a headpiece, go down on our knees, and pray. I taught her all of this, and she realised why she had been going to church all of these years.

In this church, there was a large statue of the Virgin Mary. Many people claimed that when had been to this church, they had seen the statue of the Virgin Mary move. It was a very special church.

One day, we went to church but forgot our hankies and didn't wear them on our heads. Shamiram saw a dream of the Virgin Mary shortly after this, and Mary said to her, "Ah, so you came to see me, but you did not wear your hankie on your head. I don't like that!" When Shamiram was telling me about these dreams, I was quietly excited but scared at the same time. How could she be dreaming about these things, and they seemed so real?

The messages in her dream were not symbolic. They were matter-of-fact. She kept seeing the Virgin Mary in her dreams after she fasted for three days. It was as though we had opened up the gates to spirituality for us all.

After Shamiram had the operation on her wrist to remove her tattoo, Mary was coming to her in her dreams telling her that she needed to go and sleep in the church. Mary came to her dream one night and said to her, "I want you to go and sleep in the church overnight." I agreed that we should go and speak to the priest in the hope that he would allow her to stay in the church. "Perhaps Mary wants to see you face to face."

We went to the priest, and he declined our request. He said he could not allow this to happen. I wasn't sure what to do. After this, Mary came to Shamiram in her dreams again and demanded that she go and speak to the priest. Her exact words were, "Go and tell the priest that I said you need to sleep in the church!" We went back to the priest and spoke to him again, and once again he denied us.

The third time, Jesus Christ came to Shamiram and said, "Go and tell the priest that he better allow you to sleep in that church, because my mother is very angry, and if he doesn't allow her to sleep in the church, my mother is going to do something very bad to him. This time he will say yes."

We approached the priest for the third time, and this time he agreed. He said, "OK, after mass, she is allowed to come here. She is not allowed to stay overnight; she can lie down for a couple of hours." So we agreed. We still don't know why he said yes. We knew priests didn't believe in these types of messages and dreams.

At this stage, Shamiram was still bandaged up and in excruciating pain from her tattoo removal procedure. This one particular day, we went to Mass. The priest said that she would be allowed to lay down for a couple of hours, but she could not sleep. She lay down.

When I went back to pick her up, she was a different person. When I saw her, it was like looking at somebody else. I knew she had seen something in the church. When I went to pick her up, upon walking into the church, I felt a cold shiver. A strong chilly shiver, but it was not cold. I felt like crying. I had a strange overwhelming sensation of needing to cry.

As soon as Shamiram saw me, she said to me, "We're not going to say anything to the priest, we just need to thank him and leave. I'll tell you in the car." So I agreed, and we left. It was well after midnight when I picked her up.

We got into the car, and Shamiram began to explain to me what had happened. She said, "Ishtar, you dropped me off, I was listening to the prayers within the church, and I was looking at this beautiful statue of Mary. As I was listening to the prayers in the background, the statue of Mary lifted her hand up and moved her thumb and little finger together into the position to show me three fingers: her index, middle, and ring fingers. She was giving me a signal. In the name of the father, the son, and the holy spirit (three fingers). She was blessing everybody in the church. Only I could see this, nobody else saw this.

So I asked her, "What happened after that?"

Shamiram continued, "The priest closed the door, and he left through the side doors. I stretched out on the carpet in front of the statue of Mary. I couldn't lie down on the seating. It's made of wood, and I would be sore."

Around the statue and on either side of the side of the church there is an area where you can light a candle and make a prayer. She lit a candle and lay down. Shamiram continued, "I heard a *click, click, click* sound. Three clear clicks like somebody was clicking their fingers at me as I was falling asleep. I heard *click, click, click* again and looked up. Nobody was in sight.

"I got up and looked around. Nobody was there. The priest was gone, and everybody was gone. I went and lay down again, and I felt like you do when you sit on your leg and you can't feel it?" She was trying to describe the feeling of numbness. Her whole body had become numb. It was as if she had died. She couldn't move or feel anything.

"All of a sudden, I heard somebody say, 'Wake up,' but I looked up and all I could see was a bright light. It was so bright that it was blinding. It was piercing. I had to cover my eyes to face in the direction of the light. I had to keep closing my eyes."

Shamiram heard a woman's voice say, "I'm glad you came, and thank Ishtar for this." Somehow she knew my name. She liked my name for some reason. She saw how scared Shamiram was to look into the light and said, "Don't worry, it's just the light," and Mary revealed herself wearing all white, draped clothing. She looked at Shamiram and asked, "Are you cold?"

Shamiram said yes. She wasn't scared. She didn't know what was happening or what was going on, so she had nothing to be scared of. The spirits always come to innocent people and to people who are pure. They will not reveal themselves or give messages to sinners.

Shamiram continued describing what had happened to her. "The light began to dim, and it was easier to see. The woman came towards me and covered me with a blanket so I could stay warm. She wrapped it all around me, and I felt as though I had a heater on me. It was as though I had been wrapped in an electric blanket. She then fixed my hair. I had my hankie on my head, and she fixed it. She tucked all of my hair in and tied the hankie on my head like a grandmother."

Mary then said to her, "I'm very glad you came to see me. I've been looking forward to seeing you for a long time." Mary grabbed Shamiram's hand and, relieved, said to her, "I'm glad you took this away from your hand. That was done to you when you were a child. A woman did this to you on purpose to hurt you. She was evil."

Mary looked at her hand and said, "Are you in pain?" Shamiram said yes. Mary turned her hand and gripped onto where her bandages were from her operation. Shamiram said that once she did this, the pain instantly disappeared. Shamiram had been in such excruciating pain that she was on medications and painkillers for it, but they were not concealing the pain at all. But now the pain was gone.

Mary said to her, "You are going back to Iraq. You are not staying in this country, but don't worry, Ishtar will help you to do that. You will go back to see your brother who passed on."

Shamiram's brother had tragically died in the army in Iraq while she was living in Australia. She had never forgiven herself for not being around and close by when her brother died, because they were so close and she loved her brother so much.

Mary continued, "You will go and see him, just as you see me. Like a ghost. Tell Ishtar not to say anything to the priest and that I will always look after her no matter where she is or what she is doing, I will always be there, because she did a good thing looking after you. Don't tell anybody what has happened except Ishtar, because nobody will believe you. You will see me again. I will tell you when to come. Just give the priest something but don't tell him anything, because he doesn't believe either. When you see the woman who did this to you, don't tell her anything."

I was still engaged to Costa at this time. Mary said to Shamiram, "Tell Ishtar, this is not the ring that she will be wearing. She will have another ring." Not long after, I left Costa.

When I walked into the church, I knew something had happened. I felt a strange energy or a power come over me. It was as if the holy spirit had fallen on me.

After leaving Costa, I planned to go to America. My aunty was there, and so I was planning on going to stay with her. Jesus came to Shamiram in her dream. He knocked on the door and came into my house and sat on the same chair that I always sit. I'm a creature of habit; I always sit in the same spot. Shamiram said she knew him as a familiar face but didn't know who he was. He was sitting on my chair and was crying. His tears were dropping on the carpet—in fact, pouring on the carpet.

Shamiram went and opened him a new box of tissues and went to give it to him, and as she handed him the tissue box she caught a glimpse of his hand and saw the hole in his hand, and she knew who he was instantly. When he saw that, he closed his hands straight away and pulled away suddenly. It was as if he did not want her to see it or know who he was.

He turned to Shamiram and said, "Tell Ishtar I'm not sending her where she wants to go to her aunty. She's not going there. Just tell her she's not going there." I wondered why and could not make sense of all of this. It was as if we were living in another time zone. All of these visits and conversations were happening so quickly, within close proximity, and more frequently over a short period of time.

Meanwhile, I asked Shamiram how her hand was, and it had completely healed within a week of her procedure—immediately after her first encounter with Mary. Shamiram had been to see her doctor for a check-up, and the doctor couldn't understand how it had healed so quickly. He was puzzled. It takes months for this sort of wound to heal. Shamiram was no longer taking any painkillers or antibiotics. It had completely healed.

In another dream, the Virgin Mary visited Shamiram and said to her, "I want you to come and see me at the church again. But this time come before the sunset." Sunset is at five o'clock, and five o'clock is when the prayers happen. When Shamiram told me this, I turned to her and said, "Oh my God! I think she's going to give you something." I'm still not sure how and why I knew or felt this. I was too scared to admit that I was predicting these events and feeling what was going on. I was in denial.

I encouraged Shamiram to go to church as requested by Mary. It was a Saturday about a week after her first encounter. I was at Shamiram's house looking after her son while she was out at church, and I was ironing some clothes for her. Shamiram came back home, and she had the biggest smile on her face. She was so excited. She had rosary beads in her hand. They were exactly the same ones as in an image of Mary with rosary beads around her neck.

The rosary beads had a distinct aroma, like something I had never smelt before. I asked her where she got this from. She said, "Mary came out of the light again. It was a piercing bright light, and I couldn't see very well. She came out of the light, took the rosary beads off, put them around my neck, and told me to give them to people who believe and they will heal. She told me to take it with me to Iraq and give it to your father. She said to leave my son here. 'Don't worry,' she said, 'Ishtar will look after him. I want you to go back to Iraq. You don't belong here. You're not ready to be in this country. Ishtar will help you to go back.'" This all happened prior to the war between the United States and Iraq in the 1990s.

I asked Shamiram again where she got these beads from. She told me Mary gave them to her. I said to her, "You're not lying about this?"

She replied, "No Ishtar, I swear, she gave them to me and said take them back to Iraq, give them to people who believe, and make sure I give them to your father."

I took the beads from her and placed them around my neck. I was instantly overcome with a strange electric energy. It lasted so long. It went all the way past my knee. The cross sat past my knee at the end of the chain. Mary was so tall, this sat perfectly on her. There was no way that these rosary beads came from anywhere else. They definitely belonged to the Virgin Mary. The beads were made of a very old wood. They were shiny and solid.

My friend Debbie came over after church and saw the beads for herself. She picked them up and immediately dropped them and said, "Oh my God, take it! This is very powerful. I can't hold it." The energy of the beads is only compatible with a true believer.

The beads didn't like Debbie. She thought she was a believer, but she wasn't.

At this stage, I had about $3,000 that I had saved up for my trip to America to start my new life. I had sold all of my furniture, which contributed to this sum, and I had my brand-new suitcases ready to go. Now Shamiram started to make plans to leave for Iraq. It was amazing how in the blink of an eye, her passport was ready as well as her visa to travel. Everything happened in a flash. She went in a flash. I gave her the $3,000, and she took it with her. I gave her this money to give to my family.

She gave the rosary beads to my father. He was a strong believer, and he slept with the beads under his pillow. Meanwhile, I was looking after my son and Shamiram's son. Eventually I contacted her son's father and had him take his son back into his care, as I couldn't look after the two boys on my own.

Three months later, my father was diagnosed with a brain tumour. The money I sent contributed to my father's funeral. Nobody had money to bury my father. I knew my family would need that money, but I had no idea that I would be paying for his funeral. When my father was on his deathbed, my mother told me that all he kept saying was, "Mary, Mary, Mary." Not Jesus, not God, just Mary.

When I found out that my father was sick and dying, I borrowed $5,000 from the bank to go and see him, and I could not go. In the meantime, I was staying with my friend Toula and her husband, Esha—I used to call him my bodyguard. This was after I had left Costa, and I was looking for a place to live. I went to the church and prayed and kept asking why God was doing this to me. Why was he taking my father away from me?

My friend and her husband knew that I was going to the church and praying. Toula was a strange character. She never had any religious images in her house. She went to see her mum one day and found a picture of Mary and took it from her mum's house and hung it up in her house. Toula was not very religious. She didn't believe. She used to stay up late, go to sleep in the early hours of the morning, and wake up in the afternoon. This was her normal routine.

Toula started playing with some tarot cards. I told her not to play with these cards, as it was no good. I used to use normal playing cards.

One night, Toula had the living daylights scared out of her. I was sleeping in the room next door, but I had left my door open. Toula saw a very bright light, and a woman wearing all white came towards her. She said that the light was like a beam—blinding almost. She heard the light speak, saying to her, "Wake up, wake up."

Toula looked into the light and said, "Who are you?"

She heard a response: "I am the one which you do not believe in. Go and close that door." The woman was pointing to the door of the room that I slept in.

Toula got up and closed my bedroom door. She asked again, "Who are you?"

Mary responded, "I am the one that you do not believe in."

"Then why are you here?"

Mary replied, "I am here for Ishtar, not for you!"

Toula replied, "Ishtar is the room next door."

Mary responded, "Ishtar already knows I exist. She believes in me. You don't. But I need you to give her a message."

Toula got argumentative. "Why don't you give her the message yourself?"

Mary insisted, "No, you will pass on this message. Tell her I cannot help her father. I am there to ease his pain, but I cannot stop him from dying. That is God's will." That is why my father kept calling out Mary's name.

Toula argued with Mary further, "Why aren't you letting Ishtar go to see her father? Why are you stopping her?"

Mary responded, "Don't you listen to the news? I'm not allowing her to go. I'm going to keep her safe where she belongs."

At this time, there were airplane hijackings, bombings, and more dangers. "But you should let her go," Toula insisted. "She wants to see her father. She loves her father, she wants to see him."

Mary said, "No, I'm not letting her go. It's too dangerous. Her father is going to be all right; I'm there to ease his pain. I will make sure he will be all right. And stop playing with those cards that you're playing with. It's not good."

Toula countered, "But Ishtar plays with cards."

Mary replied, "Yes, but Ishtar knows what she is doing. You don't know what you're doing."

Toula woke up then and couldn't sleep. She was wide awake waiting for me to wake up.

I woke up around seven, and there was Toula, eyes wide open ready to chew my ear off about her encounter with Mary. She started rambling and rushing through her conversation, trying to get everything out at once and stumbling over her words. She'd open her mouth to try to tell me what happened, and she would stutter.

I turned to her and said, "What's the matter with you, crazy woman? Stop it!"

She then started, "Oh, this is what happened." She started to tell me that Mary came to her and said all of these things.

I looked at her like she was insane. "You're mucking around with me. Is there a camera on me or something? Am I on *Candid Camera?*"

She looked at me and said, "Ishtar, I swear to God, I'm not lying to you. I've never experienced anything like this in my life!"

Toula had been diagnosed with cancer prior to this, and somehow without any treatment, she was cancer-free after this dream. She and her husband were married for years and were trying to conceive, but they had been unsuccessful for many years.

I looked at Toula after her dream, and I said to her, "You're going to have a daughter. You must make sure that you call her Mary." Not long after, she fell pregnant with her first child, a little girl, and she made sure to call the child Mary.

I was meant to go to her house. I was taken in her direction to give her new energy and life as a gift from God. Mary was everywhere with me, by my side.

I went to the church that night and I prayed. I said, "God, if you can really hear me and Mary really wants to help me, please take my father now. Don't let him suffer anymore." At that exact moment that I was praying, my father passed away. I released him. He wasn't going because he was waiting for me. My mother had told me that his eyes were constantly on the door waiting for me. He could no longer speak, he had deteriorated, and he was losing one sense at a time. The tumour had consumed his body.

At that particular time, it was quite late at night in Melbourne, and it was daytime in Iraq, it was in the afternoon. When he died, it was as if there was nothing wrong with him. His colouring went back to normal, he got a burst of energy, and it was as if this illness was not in his body. He looked fresh and vibrant. It was his last burst of life, and then he went.

This is when my world completely shattered. Nothing mattered anymore. Ashur came to see me along with many other friends and family to offer their condolences. I hated Ashur at this stage. I blamed him. It was his fault. He had caused this to happen to me. I started yelling at him, "Look at what you've done. I left my father behind for you, I left my family." I hated him more than ever after this.

Not long after, I moved out of Toula's house and into my own place. Toula helped me find the place. Mary came to her in a dream and had already chosen my home for me. Mary said to Toula, "There are two places that you are looking at for Ishtar, but one of them in particular, I would really like her to go there." She had chosen for me! I moved in very quickly after that.

Everywhere I would go and live, everybody else around me was receiving messages for me through their dreams. The messages were not coming directly to me. My closest friends and loved ones would receive messages through their dreams and pass on the messages to me.

I had the dream again of Jesus taking me up the stairs, and I knew I was having a son. We were walking up long stairs. It was like a theatre staircase. I never thought I would have another child after having a second abortion at three months. My cousin had seen my baby son in a basinet in her dream.

MEETING MY SECOND HUSBAND

My father came to Toula in her dreams. She said he was wearing all white. He said to her in her dream, "Tell Ishtar I love her very, very much. Tell her not to worry that she didn't come to see me."

She came to me and said she had a dream. She began to describe her dream: "This man came looking for you. He was wearing a red sweater and jeans. He was looking around the Brunswick area. He came to my house and said, 'Where is Ishtar? I am looking for her.' I stuttered and couldn't get my words out clearly, and just as I was going to tell him where you were, he spotted you. He saw you, came to you, and gave you a card." I could make no sense of her dream but I listened anyway.

That particular night, we were all going out to a club called Lazar in the city. We went on a regular basis, but this night in particular I really didn't want to go. My friend had passes to get in and insisted that we go. There was three of us altogether, and I was almost dragged into the place.

We were sitting in the lounge area of the club having a drink and chatting away. I remember I was wearing a bright red, short, tailored jacket. As we were sitting minding our own business, two men walked past us. One of them tried to be a bit smart and said to us, "We are here to pick up. We're looking for a good time." I was so angry. I told him to piss off and asked him who he thought he was and who he thought he was talking to. I turned away.

The other man who was with him approached me and apologised. He said, "I apologise for my friend. He is a real idiot. Sorry."

I turned to him and said, "That's all right, don't worry about it. Just keep a leash on him. We don't need to pick up anyone."

He responded, "Ladies like yourselves, you don't need to try and pick up. Let me introduce myself. I'm Stavro." He handed me a business card with his number on it as he was introducing himself. He stood there talking to me for hours before he eventually asked if he could sit next to me. He sat and we talked some more.

The girls were excited. They were saying how nice he was and how good he was. I remember saying to them, "Let me dance with him, and I'll let you know."

Stavro and I walked to the dance floor and began to dance. I felt connected to him straight away. He was polite and was a gentleman. Suddenly, I came to the realisation that Toula had described this man to me when she had seen him in her dream. At the time, she was pregnant with her daughter who she later named Mary, and I was the godmother.

Stavro and I began to date, and I wanted to test Toula out to see how real the premonitions in her dreams really were. I asked for her to come over to my place at a particular time and gave her an excuse. I made sure it was at a time when Stavro would be over, so I could see her reaction when she saw him. Was this the man she had seen in her dreams? Toula was known for being a little bit crazy and off-centre sometimes, so I wanted to test her out.

She came my house and sat down. We chatted for a while; we were relaxed. There was a knock at the door, and Stavro walked in wearing his red sweater and jeans. She looked at him and went white. Stavro was concerned for her and asked if she was OK. He got no response out of her. It was as if she had seen a ghost.

Toula turned to me and said, "This is the man I saw in my dream!" She had described him to me previously—light-coloured eyes, mousy brown hair, his build, he wasn't very tall, everything. Stavro was puzzled and didn't know why my friend looked as if she'd seen a ghost. Before Toula left, she looked at me and said, "You're going to marry this man. I swear to God, it's the man I've seen in my dream."

After we dated for a while, I told him what had happened and about the dream. He said, "Well, actually, I was living in Brunswick before I moved to Toorak." Creepy! This was all so strange!

BRINGING MY FAMILY TO AUSTRALIA

I heard from my sisters in Iraq that the situation in the country was getting worse. My sisters would cry on the phone, desperate for me to help them get their papers sorted with immigration to have them come to Australia. At this stage, Iraq had become extremely dangerous for young women, particularly without their father. They had no man in their life to protect them, and they wanted to get out as soon as they could. I told them to leave the country and promised to help them with their papers to come to Australia the best I could.

My sisters fled Iraq and went to Jordan, where they stayed with our aunty. They called me from there, and she helped them settle in with some Palestinian people. They had a room that my three sisters shared, and they stayed there until I could arrange for them to come to Australia.

At this stage, it was my youngest sister, the fourth oldest sister, and the second oldest sister. They needed money to live as well as money to pay for flights. I spoke with my aunty in the United States who I knew had some money that she could help them with financially. I had a newborn baby as well as my older son. I wasn't working, and supporting my family was difficult enough. I wasn't able to help my sisters out financially. The best I could do was help them come to Australia and give them the opportunity to have a better quality of life and the chance at a safe and more prosperous future for themselves.

My aunty was willing and able to assist, and so she was able to support my sisters by sending them money on a monthly basis to survive. In the meantime, I was in contact with one of our priests who was quite involved in government relations and politics and was able to assist political refugees. He helped me with the immigration application process for my sisters. The whole process took some time, about a year from memory, but eventually they were able to come and stay in Australia. The Assyrian church was very helpful in making this happen.

Finally, my sisters arrived, and I could have my family together after twenty-five years. I took them on as my responsibility and had them stay with me in my home with my husband and two children. My idea was for us to all work together as a family and possibly do so by working together in our own business and buying a home all together. We could slowly expand from that point and build a better future for ourselves that way.

It obviously didn't work out the way I had imagined. My sisters began to turn against me. During this time, they were still living in my house, which meant that I was still feeding three extra mouths. There were seven of us living in my house without any contribution from anybody. They would pick on me. They wouldn't help around the house, and they demanded that I constantly go to the supermarket and make sure the house was stocked up with food and living necessities. They acted as if I owed them a favour or was obligated for some reason to them.

I was torn between my sisters and my husband and children, and I was not sure what to do. I was all over the place. My sisters and I would argue constantly. They would lock themselves in their room and not come out while I would be in the lounge room and they refused to speak to me. Awkward in your own home!

I have a medical condition with an overactive thyroid, and stress plays a big part in my general health. One particular day amongst all the arguing and fighting, I collapsed. One of my sisters accused me of being a drama queen and said I was only acting. My heart was pounding at over 180 beats per minute. It was as if I was having a heart attack. At that stage, I didn't realise that this was caused by an overactive thyroid. I was so thin that my skeletal structure should have given it away. I recall this occurring in the month of August.

August is a very holy month and a sacred one in our religion. We pray and fast during this period, and there should be love and peace during prayer and fasting periods. Rather than peace, we were constantly fighting. Fasting would have also played a part in my collapse that day. There was constant fighting and arguing between my husband and I and my sisters and I.

One night I had a dream. It was very real. It was as if I was really there. I was walking through Jerusalem, and I approached an alley-like street with small stalls along the side. It was like a market. I was wearing normal clothes, though; I wasn't wearing the clothes that they wore in Biblical times.

The stalls were all empty. There was nobody in sight. I continued walking through until I finally got to one stall, and there was a man standing there. He looked like Jesus Christ. Same eyes, same hair, same facial structure, even the same clothes and shoes. Had I found Jesus Christ in my dream? He was standing behind the stall, and he was trying to sell me something.

I thought about it and realised that Jesus doesn't like to sell things. I gazed into his eyes and said, "No, you are not Jesus."

He looked at me with a raised eyebrow and said to me in a creepy sneering voice, "Ooohhhh, what do you mean?"

He was looking at me in a devilish way, and I said to him again, "You're not Jesus Christ."

He let out a great big echoing evil laugh like "Mwah ha ha ha." This scared me. I was frightened. I began to back off slowly and kept backing up until I could find a way to get away from him.

As I was looking for an escape, a set of stairs appeared before me, and it was as if I needed to leave up these stairs. The echo of his laughter continued through my panic up the stairs. He was still laughing at me. I kept running up these stairs. It felt like forever. I found myself running up onto a hill. Lush greenery was all around me, and all of a sudden, there were people everywhere.

Everybody was dressed in old-fashioned clothing—the robe-like clothing that we see in icons in the church and that we envision. I felt strange coming across all of these people dressed this way. Everybody was standing around listening to somebody speak. I was pushing and shoving and ducking and weaving through the crowd, wanting to see why all of these people were standing around. Who were they looking at? What were they doing? Who were they listening to? And why were they there?

Finally, huffing and puffing, I made it to the front. I looked up, and I saw Jesus Christ standing on a hill. His palms were open facing upward and outwards as if to embrace all of the people, and there he was preaching. I looked at him, and his eyes met mine. As soon as he saw me, he closed his palms so I could not see his old wounds. Having seen that, I knew he was the real deal.

Jesus said to me, "You knew it. You knew it wasn't me, and I know you know who I am. But I don't have time for you right now. So get away from the evil."

I had no idea what this meant. It was as if he was keeping an eye on me and he wanted to help me, but he didn't have time to spend with me at that point in time. He had too many people to look after. I woke up suddenly, eyes wide open like an owl.

A few days following this dream, I asked my sisters to leave my house. I told them they needed to move out. The evil was amongst us, but I didn't know who it was or where it was coming from, so the best thing to do was to remove my sisters from my home to begin with.

When my sisters left, I was not home. This whole ordeal hurt me so deeply. I hadn't seen my family for so long, and after twenty-five years, I was treated this way by them. I felt as though a knife was taken and pierced straight through my heart. I felt abandoned and betrayed.

I sought therapy after this ordeal because I needed closure. I needed to understand whether this was my wrongdoing or there was something I could do to change the situation. My therapist told me that I hadn't done anything apart from being kind and caring, and that I had to do whatever was necessary to bring my family together. My therapist reassured me that wanting my family to be together after so long was not a bad thing; however, it seemed that unfortunately I was simply their free meal ticket into Australia.

My therapist said that they probably thought I had a lot of money and could look after them, and once they saw that this was not the case and they could not freeload off of me, it frustrated them. He helped me see that what I thought they were thinking was quite likely what they were in fact thinking. I didn't really want them to go, but it just had to happen. There was far too much tension, fighting, and negativity around us.

At this point in my life, I was so lost. I was unsure of what my direction was. I was still finding myself. My husband wasn't working much. He was working part-time as a waiter, but he was not making much money, and financially and spiritually I was looking for direction.

At the same time, my mother and other sisters left Iraq for Australia also. At this point, my sisters helped them to come here, as they were now permanent residents of the country. I tried to help as much as I could and organised their papers also. My mother and other sisters stayed in Iraq until they were granted their visas and entry into Australia.

Although my sisters had acted this way towards me, I thought my mother would be different. Perhaps if she came here, she would be able to babysit my child so I could go to work part-time and make some money. That didn't happen either.

The sister who was with my mum was losing her speech, and nobody had any idea what was wrong with her. Within two days of her being in Australia, I had her booked in with doctors and specialists. I was taking her from doctor appointment to appointment, trying to help her as much as I could. I was the only one in the family who spoke decent English, and so I took it upon myself to help. I was able to talk with the doctors and act as an interpreter. After going back and forth from doctor to doctor, finally we made an appointment to see a specialist in neurosurgery. He ran countless scans and tests, and it was confirmed that my sister had a brain tumour. Action needed to be taken immediately. It was a matter of urgency, and so I pushed for her surgery to be as soon as possible. She was taken in for surgery very soon thereafter.

In my upbringing, in our culture, and particularly in my family, we have always had a strong belief in a higher power—something much stronger than any man who has walked this earth and stronger than any structure either natural or manmade that resides on this earth. I am still not sure why, but this belief is particularly strong in me and has been from a young age. In our religion and with faith instilled in a higher power, we believe that miracles do happen. When I have ever asked for something, it does happen. I prayed constantly for my sister, and I fasted for three days prior to her surgery.

On the day of her surgery, I went to the hospital, and I was waiting. I was there on my own. I had told the rest of my family not to come to the hospital until the surgery was complete and she was in recovery. I knew how stressful it would be and how much more tension would have been created if they were there. While my sister was in surgery, I paced the hallway up and down and prayed continuously.

When the doctor came out of the surgery, I heard his voice saying, "Come here, Ishtar, I need to speak with you."

In a panic I rushed over. "Is she OK?"

He continued, "She is fine. Can I ask you something?" He stared at me puzzled and wondering how he would make sense of what he was about to say to himself, let alone to me. "I'm a man of science, and I find it strange to ask you … do you have a guardian angel?"

My jaw dropped. "Doctor, how could you possibly believe in guardian angels? What do you know about this sort of thing?"

He looked at me so deeply puzzled. "Well, Ishtar, let me tell you something. When we go into this type of surgery, we are supposed to simply open the skull and take a specimen from the tumour to determine what it is. We run tests. When we opened your sister's skull, it was drawn for us. There was an outline around the area that needed to be removed.

"When I was holding my tools and in particular my scalpel to cut a specimen from the tumour, it was as if somebody was holding my hand. I felt nothing. I could see the movement of my hand, and it followed the outline, but it was as if my hand was guided by someone. It was completely cleaned, and the entire tumour was removed. Not one bit of any other part aside from the tumour was touched.

"Once the cut was complete and the tumour was cut out, I felt the presence of my hand again and regained full movement and control of my hand. I felt a presence in the room, and it was as if somebody was standing right behind me moving my hand."

I smiled and said to him, "Well, doctor, we do believe in a higher power."

He continued, "When we closed up the surgery and were ready for stitches, that is when my hand movement was back to normal. The operation was successful and completed very quickly. We also ran tests on the tumour removed, and it was malignant. She would have died within a month or two had this not been attended to."

I thanked the doctor for all that he had done. When my sister came out of surgery, she was taken into the intensive care unit for around-the-clock observation. The doctors and nurses began to question her: Where are you? What day is it? What is your name? What city are we in? What's just happened to you? Without any hesitation, my sister began to rattle off, "I'm in the Royal Melbourne Hospital, it's Tuesday, my name is ..., we are in Melbourne, I've just had brain surgery." She was answering everything without any problems.

The doctors continued. "Can you feel your legs?" "Yes!" and she would move them. "Can you feel this pressure on your hands?" "Yes!" She would move her fingers and arms. When I went to see her in the ICU (where most patients can barely move and are in critical condition), she was sitting up in her bed as if it was just another day and nothing had happened.

"Where are my sisters? Where is my mother? Why aren't they here?" she began to question me.

"They are all on their way, don't worry. How do you feel?" I responded.

"I feel great!"

The only way that I can explain this whole situation is that it was a miracle from a higher power. My prayers were heard and answered. Scientifically and in medical terms, there is no way to explain how this whole ordeal could be possible. My sister had lost her speech, and her health was deteriorating so rapidly. Within two days of her arriving in the country, I had her booked in with doctors, specialists, and surgeons. Not long after, it was determined that she had a fatal cancer that was going to take her life within a couple of months at most. Somehow, the surgery was moved forward out of a sense of urgency. And then there's the surgeon's description of what he saw (the outline of what needed to be removed) and felt (no sensation during the surgery and regaining sensation once the tumour was removed). Then we consider her recovery: as soon as she woke up, it was as if nothing had happened to her, and she was sitting up in her hospital bed wondering why she was still there.

She was discharged from hospital within two days. This was most certainly a miracle. I am sure of it!

STORIES FROM MY GRANDMOTHER

When I growing up, my grandmother used to tell me lots of stories. One of the stories was that there was a woman who never went to church. She used to pray at home in the corner of her house. People passed her house, and they would ask why she never went to church. They started to tell her that God wouldn't accept her prayers at home—she must go to church and pray.

The woman believed what people were telling her. She questioned her own beliefs, thinking maybe God was not listening to her prayers and she must go to church. So she went to the church, and she saw all these people carrying some sort of a sack on their back—it looked something like a Santa Claus sack that he would carry on his shoulder with all the presents inside it. The priest's sack was the largest.

She looked around. She didn't have anything, and she felt that she needed to do the same as the others were doing. She grabbed something that she found near her, and she carried it on her shoulder like she saw everyone else doing.

An angel appeared to her only and said to her, "What are you doing, woman?"

She said, "I have to come to the church to pray because God cannot accept my prayers at home. I want to make sure that God hears my prayers."

The angel said to her, "Do you know what they are carrying on their back?"

She said no.

The angel said to her, "Why did you do the same thing that they do?"

She said, "I have to follow what they are doing. Isn't this what I am supposed to be doing, following the rules of the church?"

He said to her, "These people are carrying their sins on their back. God is listening to your prayers, so go home and keep on doing what you were doing—praying at home. Don't listen to what other people tell you to do. It has nothing to do with the church; it needs to be felt within. It means you believe in your heart and in your soul. So in other words, when you believe, it comes from within, and it has nothing to do with the building, God is everywhere and is listening to you wherever you are. Whether you are inside or out in the garden, you are surrounded by his energy. We are surrounded by it, and God exists through us."

This is one of the stories my grandmother told me. Some I remember, some I don't. I feel sad and frustrated when people ask me why God punishes good people. That's not true; God only teaches us a lesson in life so we can grow up to be strong and survive. I know and you know we are here for a reason. We must find the reason why we are here. I found my reason, and I know you can too. If you are strong and open-minded and you have an open heart, you will find it, but you have to be open to it. I asked myself the same question about why God has punished me. I can get the answer because God only speaks through you. That is why I never lost my faith.

I will give you another story; maybe this one will make more sense to you. The story is of the angel of death, he takes the soul, he feels no remorse. God said to him, "Go down to earth, there is a soul I need you to bring to me."

So, Angel of death went down to earth and looked at the young man. He was so happy with his family, and Angel of death felt sorry for him and didn't want to take his life from his family. Angel of death could not go back to God empty-handed, so he looked at the next-door neighbour, an old man ninety years old who was ready to die. Angel of death took the older man's soul and gave it to God.

God said to Angel of death, "What is this? I did not send you down to bring me this soul."

Angel of death said, "But my Lord, the young soul you sent me to get has young children and is happy with his life. I felt sorry for this young soul."

God sent Angel of death to take this young soul three times, but Angel of death just could not do it. He could not understand why God was sending him to take this young soul when this soul looked so happy.

Finally, God said to Angel of death, "Come with me. Have a look at this field of flowers. I want you to go out there, and I want you to bring me the flower you feel that I deserve."

Angel of death went and looked around the field. He took his time looking for the right flower that God deserved. He didn't want to pick one that was too open or one that just didn't look right. He felt he had to pick the kind of flower that when you look at it, it is just perfect—the stem is right, the colour is right, the way the flower looked is perfect. That is what he wanted to give to God: the perfect flower.

Angel of death picked such a flower and presented it to God, saying, "This is the right one. This is the one you deserve."

God questioned why Angel of death had picked this particular flower.

"Lord, I could not see anything that was suitable for you, but this one was perfect."

God questioned Angel of death as to whether he understood what God wanted for his garden. Angel of death then saw that what God meant was that the young soul was perfect in his garden and that he deserved it. The young soul was still growing, he was a good person, and he had no bad sins. The old man was a sinner, and in God's eyes the old man needed to be tested more on earth. The old man had to cleanse his soul first—in other words, turn to God first so God could forgive him and take him away.

God said, "I am the fire that you cannot shut off or turn down. If you come closer and question me in a bad way, I will burn you quicker than you think it will happen to you." In other words, people who question God will be tested. You are not being punished; he is trying to tell you something, but you have to figure out what he is trying to tell you and what you have done to deserve this test. You need to ask yourself, "What have I done?" In other words, whatever you do on earth, you will pay for it (karma). Remember, what you do to others will be done to you. The wheel is always in motion. It is always moving. We are all equal in the eyes of God.

We have been given a choice in life. We have the willpower to be happy or unhappy. We get confused—lost in our mind. The mind is very powerful thing; it can be manipulated by the demon in our weakest moments. When we are weak, the demon feeds on your power. You must listen more to yourself, take a moment, and listen within. The answers are within.

Have faith in yourself. You are capable of making things happen, but we have so little faith in ourselves. We all are born with some sort of a gift; we must search inside ourselves and find what gift we have been given, what we are capable of doing for ourselves. Once you find what has been given to you, hold onto it. We all have a purpose in life. We are all special in our own way.

It took me a long time to try to figure out what my gift is. I was tested through my life to finally figure out what my purpose in life was. It was not an easy road, but with my faith, I was guided there—and to this day I still am.

MY FATHER AND HIS BELIEF

My father was not a religious person, but he had lots of faith. He never went to church, not even for wedding or funerals. However, my father read the whole Bible from the beginning to the end. He always used to make me read the Bible to my sisters, and he used to explain what it meant, as I was too young to understand.

I learned a lot from him, because belief is in your heart. Attending church doesn't mean that you are a believer. Church is a symbol. Why I am saying this? From my experience, I have seen people who attend church proclaim that they believe in God, but as soon as they come out of the building, they talk about each other. They have just come out of church, and they have already started to have bad thoughts about people. I have witnessed a lot of this.

I just shake my head and think that God does not want this. We should respect each other. Learn to forgive before you go to church. It does not matter how bad the other person was towards you. If you are going inside that building, and if you are going to take communion, you need to be pure inside your heart and soul. Church is not just a building, it is a symbol of God, and you need to respect him.

God is in our souls and minds always. There are no rules. What you feel, whether you love him or not—that has to be your choice. We lose ourselves in everyday life by thinking how we can buy a house and pay for it, how we are going to send our children to school and pay for their education, what kind of car we should buy. These are all materialistic things in life.

We are not less to God than the bird that flies every day and eats and sleeps and is happy. So if God is looking after that bird, we are more important to God than that bird. In other words, God will provide for us.

We won't be taking anything with us when our time is up. We are visitors here. Some people call us aliens. We are here on borrowed time. The only thing we take with us is our memories.

People come to me for guidance, and I try my best to show them the way it is meant to be and understand it. We work with it. Take the good and bad together in your life. It does become easier and more balanced.

I'm sure we all get frustrated and angry and then we lose our way and start making wrong decisions to escape. Some people get addictions like alcohol, drugs, and gambling. That's when you are weakest in your mind, and it is easier to escape your reality than face it.

I made a lot of mistakes in my life. I do regret many things. If only I'd had someone to guide me and help me in my path, I would have done things differently. We cannot dwell on the past, but we can learn from it and grow up from our experience. We can teach our children and others, and maybe they will learn from our mistakes and not do the same things we did. Unfortunately, that's life. We need to learn from our mistakes and hopefully grow.

I always ask God to give me the strength and the energy and faith to continue my journey in this life and not lose my way. We have to be realistic but also must open our mind to anything and everything this life gives us.

When I came to Australia, I was so happy and excited to build my life with my husband and my child. I did not think that I was going do all of it on my own. Unfortunately, my husband chose the wrong path. I know we were too young to get married. Maybe it was my way of escaping the difficult life I had growing up, or it was my destiny to come to this country and give a chance to my family to come here and build their life, to save them from Iraq and the government and the war.

I am proud to have given my family the life they needed, even though when they came to Australia they turned against me. That's all right. I know in my heart I did the right thing. When you do something for others, do not expect anything back. That's not the way life is. If you expect something back, you will be disappointed.

When I do something for others, I know that my reward will come from a higher power. Expect the unexpected, and you won't be disappointed and hurt. I'm sure you have been through it yourself. That's why I need to express myself in this book. When you do read it, you will relate to me because every one of us has some sort of experience.

MY GRANDFATHER

Now I'd like to talk about my grandfather. He was in World War II. My grandfather was a great man, a brave man, and a loving and caring man, but when it came to his family, he was very hard person to live with. I heard a lot of stories about my grandfather, but I know that he was good to me, loved me, cared for me, and raised me in every way like his daughter, not granddaughter. We were very close.

My grandfather was shocked when his son enlisted in the army. He knew what the army could do to a person. He saw so much that he knew it could destroy you. Psychologically, you could come back a different person. He has been there and done that. After he saw two men come to his front door dressed up like military police to pick my uncle up because he'd escaped from the army, my grandfather went blind. He could not see anything anymore.

He used to stay at home in his bed. He only heard voices. He knew by the voice who they were. I used to go and visit my grandmother and my grandfather in their house. When he heard my voice, he used to call me and hug me and kiss me. I used to feel so sorry for him, because he was hopeless and frustrated. He was always happy to hear my voice when I visited him.

He could not do anything for his family. He felt like he was less of a man. I'm sure that's what he felt. It's hard for any man not to help his family, not to work, not to see his grandchildren grow up and be there for them.

My grandmother used to clean him, give him a bath, and look after him in every way she could. That was my grandmother's life, her destiny, to do what she needed to do for her family. Life wasn't easy for them. I'm sure she was very frustrated too and felt hopeless. That is the test of life—the twists and turns—but you must have faith no matter what.

My uncle was the third child in the family. He was young; we used to call him the rebel without a cause because he was always getting himself in trouble. When he went into the army, he was even more in trouble because he could not stay long enough to serve in the army. He was always escaping, and then they'd find him and he would be court-martialled. He would be put in prison. Certain times he was let out of prison to go back to the army and serve his time. The army was only for one year, but it turned out to be five years. I loved my uncle, but he was always in trouble.

Then he fell in love with this young girl, like the story of Romeo and Juliet. She loved him like a soulmate. She was willing to run away with him because her family did not approve of my uncle. They knew how troubled he was. They were worried for their daughter that he wasn't going to treat her right and love her, and he was still in the army. That didn't stop them from being together.

He came to my father and asked my father to help him with this girl, as he wanted to marry her. My father said, "What do you want me to do about it?"

My uncle said, "We are going to run away together and get married. I asked for her hand in marriage, and they refused."

My father said, "OK then." He told my aunty and my uncle and the younger ones, "You have to go to the house and give her the sign to come out outside." He waited for them to come back from picking her up at the house by taxi. She stayed with us until my uncle came out from the army so we could start the ceremony.

Their marriage all happened so fast. I remember it like a dream. Everybody was in our house, and they were preparing for something. I did not understand much of it, as I was so young no one was telling me anything. All I know was my uncle came from the army dressed up in his uniform. I was so happy to see him, and I was happy to see the girl who became my aunty. She was happy to see him too.

My father went to get the priest to marry, them but the priest refused. He wanted the consent of her parents. My father said to him, "What are you talking about? The girl just ran away to be with my brother, so you have to marry them without her parents' consent."

My father's cousin was there too. He was a nice tall handsome man with blue eyes, and he always looked after my father. He was always there to protect and look after my father. My dad needed his help as they were growing up together. They had protected each other since they were children, and so when the priest was arguing with my father and my father started arguing and was very angry with the priest, his cousin got involved.

The cousin said to the priest, "I will shoot you if you don't." He always carried a gun with him no matter where he went for protection, and he was not afraid of anything. This man was very brave, very strong, and very tall. He had five girls and one boy, so that is why he used to carry a gun—to protect his daughters.

The priest knew that he meant business, so he went ahead and did the ceremony. Before the ceremony, my father asked my uncle, "Do you have money to get married?"

He said no, so my father had to pay for the ceremony and the wedding. They invited a few people, and then her parents found out what was happening. They came over to our house, and they were very upset and angry at their daughter for what she had done. It was too late to undo it now, though.

So my aunty and my uncle stayed with us in our house for a while until my uncle finish his time in the army. In the meantime, my mother used to teach this young girl how to clean and do laundry and become a woman of the house. She learned a lot from my mother and used to listen a lot.

She was a good aunty, and l liked her a lot. She was like a child. She used to play with me all the time. When they left my house, I was devastated, because I had become so close to them in that period of time. I felt that every time I got close to someone, they went away. I am sure they felt the same thing about leaving me.

After they left, they lived with my grandmother. Later, while they were living together with my other uncle, she got pregnant, and my aunty gave birth to a baby girl. The baby was so beautiful. My grandmother used to look after the baby and care for her. At the time, my grandfather was still alive.

Then my grandfather died a very horrible death. It started with fire in his bed. My grandmother wasn't there because she was outside chasing my little cousin, who was only two years old, inside the house. Only when she saw smoke coming out of the window did she realise that my grandfather was on fire. She ran inside and threw water all over him to stop the fire from spreading everywhere in the house.

The ambulance came and took my grandfather to the hospital to try to save him, but it was too late. His body was burned badly, and there was no way to save him. My grandmother told me that with his last breath, he was asking for me. I was too far away to be there, plus I was very young at the time. He would be a nightmare for me to see. I wanted to have his good memories in my mind.

I think I was eight years old when my cousin was running towards me as I came out of school. She told me the devastating news. She said, "Your father died!"

I said, "What father? Which one what are you talking about?"

She said, "Your grandfather then."

I fell to the ground. I don't remember what happened because I was so shocked. When I came around, I did not want to know that what I'd heard was true.

My father never went to the funeral, and I didn't go to the funeral either. I was too young to go. I was angry with my mother and my grandmother because they did not allow me to go to the funeral. I did not get to say goodbye to my grandfather. I used to dream about him all the time, saying goodbye in my dreams.

I remember I used to wake up and cry all the time. I could not imagine him not there for me. I thought it was only a dream and I was going to wake up and my grandfather would still be with us. That was not the case.

Finally, reality kicked in. I'm sure a lot of you have felt that way when you lose someone special in your life who was always there for you and loved you and hugged you and listened to you all the time. Great memories I have of my grandfather are always in my thoughts and in my heart forever. I will never forget him.

Time heals all wounds. You must continue your journey of life, but keep the memories of the good times, because you cannot forget you miss that special person. Of course, we believe our loved ones are in a good place, better than this place. I think of all the knowledge my grandfather and father gave me that made me who

I am. They gave me the strength to keep going in my life, to be strong and spiritual and move forward.

I had to face all the obstacles in my life and hardships, and do it all by myself without anybody's help. I had to learn in every way what life gave me, and that's how I became strong in life. When I got very stressed and lost, I sought my father for guidance and direction.

Once I was so stressed up, I was driving and talking to my father. I knew he could hear me as I begged, "Please give me answers." That night, I had a dream that my father came. He was wearing a leather jacket and jeans and a nice shirt that I had sent to him when he was alive. He came in and said to me, "What's wrong, Ishtar?"

I said, "I am so tired, Dad. I don't know what to do."

He said, "Put your head on my lap," and he started stroking my hair. I felt he had confidence in me and was giving me strength to go on. At the time, I was dealing with lots of problems in my life, trying to keep all my energy and strength for my son. My marriage was falling apart, but I could not focus on that. It was not important to me at the time.

I know my father and grandfather are looking after me from beyond. They're always there; even though I cannot see them, their spirits live on. All I have to do is ask for their spirits to come to me and guide me.

Believe and have faith that the dead are not gone—they are all around us. Try to open your mind sometimes. You don't have to see things to believe. A feeling tells you to listen to that voice inside when it is talking to you. We ignore it most of the time because we don't want to know. It scares us, and that's when we lose our faith.

When I am helping and guiding others, I chew on their energy and focus on what the energy tells me. I sensed whether the energy is good or bad, positive or negative. It is like I become the person I am doing the reading on. I feel what's going on around them, almost like I am them. It is very hard to describe what I feel. Sometimes after a day of reading, it is like I switch on and switch off.

When I feel the energy is very bad, something stops it from come in through myself. I won't allow bad energy to connect with me, no matter how strong it is. That energy means evil demons. The light is always with me; it surrounds me, and I feel it all the time. I am protected from on high. Especially when I am around people, I don't allow myself to become too close to that sort of energy. If you are a gifted psychic. medium or spiritual healer, you will feel it around you and around the people closest to you. Evil cannot hide from you.

Of the people who do this kind of work, a majority of them are fake. We all need to write answers in life to guide us and keep us safe and comfortable. We want some answers, and that's why we seek people who have the gift to help us and balance life. But there are people out there who will try to take your money and not give you any answers. I have been to people like that when I needed direction in my life and guidance. They only wanted my money. They never helped me in any way.

Maybe they couldn't get through my energy and couldn't read me at all. Maybe I went to the wrong ones. I know people take advantage of other people, but you have to be open to the spirit world to have your reading done properly. Otherwise, it won't work.

MY MOTHER

When I was a young child, I would go outside in the street and use my imagination to play. I used to gather lots of rocks, and I used to pretend I had a shop selling rock melons. People used to go past me and laugh. They thought I was cute. I was only two years old at the time. How do I know? My grandmother used to tell me about my imagination.

I know I was a happy child while I was living with my grandmother, because she was kind, loving, and caring. When my grandmother died, I was here in Australia. I was devastated when I heard that she was gone. Unfortunately, all the good people go first. I'm sure she is in a good place now.

My happy childhood ended when I was returned to my mother. She was a very angry person. She would abuse me psychologically, mentally, emotionally, and physically. This went on until I was fifteen and started to realise that I could not stay with her. If I did, either I or she would die.

The abuse was constant. You can only take so much abuse in life, especially when you are a teenager. She called me all the names under the sun. I could not defend myself at the time. I used to cry and cry and cry. Sometimes I would go to bed hungry. I was so mentally exhausted I could not focus on my homework. I was a good student; I loved school, and it was my way of escaping her.

I used to fear going back home. Anything that was going wrong in the house, she will take it out on me, because I was the oldest one. I could not take it anymore, so one day we had a big argument. She started beating me, so I grabbed her by the hair. I did not want to let go, because I didn't want to be abused again.

She was very difficult woman to deal with. Whether you were nice or not, it did not make a difference. You could not come to some sort of compromise with this woman. Even now, she has not changed at all. She still manipulates everyone against each other and tries to create trouble between all of us sisters. I thought she would be changed after all these years, but unfortunately, that is not the case.

All I ever wanted from her was to love me. I will never get the love that I want from my mother. I do not know why. She is good with my sisters. They get along very well with each other, but I am the outsider.

You cannot make someone love you, even your own mother. She is the reason I left Iraq and got married young. She forced me to make the biggest decision of my life. Don't get me wrong; I don't regret anything. It was meant to be this way. But I was not long in this journey when someone from a higher power started guiding me all the way.

I was one year old when my parents split up. It wasn't my fault what happened between them, but I was always to blame. I was an unlucky child for her. They were happy before I came along. It's like I was the other woman or something. At first she took me with her to her parents where they lived, so I stayed with her for a while and then her mother said, "We cannot look after your daughter too. Take her back to her father. Maybe he will come back to you that way, if he cannot handle looking after his daughter."

So my mother brought me back to my other grandmother and grandfather, and she never looked back until I was returned to her at five years old. She tried many times to get back with my father, but my father would not take her back after what she had done to me, leaving me behind like I was nothing. She always says to me now that she is sorry for what she did in the past— leaving me behind—but I don't believe her when she says she was manipulated by others. I know she was young, but I was young too when I separated from my husband, and I did not leave my son behind. This is only an excuse.

She didn't care at all. She gave me away and never looked back. After she left me with my grandparents, she went to live with her sister, and she was working. She never even sent any money to look after me to my grandparents. She couldn't care less about me. That's why I always questioned her love for me.

When she had her other daughters, she treated them differently. I used to watch her at home. She would give them hugs and kisses. I used to wish she would do that for me, but it never happened. I was almost like a stepdaughter. I felt like that always. I tried so hard to please her, but it didn't work. I was not good enough for her.

I used to cry every night before I went to sleep. I felt I was the bad daughter. If anything went wrong in the house, I was to blame for it. In the end, I had to escape. That's when my husband showed up to offer me a way to escape. If I had stayed with my mother, I would have committed suicide. That's how I felt all the time.

I'm sure God had another purpose in life for me. I used to question God all the time as to why this woman who was supposed to be my mother treated me like this. What had I done to deserve this? I never did get an answer from God. God has saved me so many times in my life, and I love him for it. So if you want to understand better, that is why I left my family behind. I still forgive my mother for what she has done to me.

MY FATHER'S STORIES

My father was a gentle soul. He always cared about people. He always helped others. He would share the money he had with his family and his friends, and anyone who needed a generous, compassionate, and caring person. When he was growing up, he lived in the north of Iraq. There were English people living there at the time and military basis for the English army. When my grandfather enlisted, he served in English army. It was a very beautiful place to live in and raise children.

At that time, my grandmother was looking after the children by herself. Basically, my father was growing up without a father figure teaching and guiding him. He had to learn on his own to become a man and survive. Because he was the oldest in the family, he had two sisters and two brothers he had to look after. He was the man of the house. He had to help his mother and work, and he got involved with the wrong people. But he had to learn.

He used to tell me lots of stories as a child of when he was teenager and what he used to do. At the age of fourteen, my father learned a trade so he could work and support his family. He was very good in English, and he became very good at his job. He was proud of what he did.

My father used to travel all the time, and that is why we only saw him every three or four months. In the way, he was escaping his own psychological problems. Also to escape he used to drink a lot; sometime he wouldn't even eat food. I always knew my father wasn't happy in his life because I used to feel his sadness within, but I was too young to ask questions.

When he came home, I used to be very happy to see him, because I knew I was safe. My father always protected me from my mother when he was around. She couldn't even touch me. He used to tell me stories about his journeys.

My dad and I were very close. If I needed something from him, he would look after me and help me and give me the things I needed. We used to laugh and watch television together. He gave me the attention I needed. He knew how much I missed when I was growing without him. He really wanted to make up for the time that we lost, so every chance he had, he spent time with me, because I needed that. Of course he loved my sisters, but I was a very special girl to him because of what I went through.

My dad was my soulmate. I loved him so much, and I appreciated the attention. He was a responsible man, a caring man, and a spiritual man full of joy and laughter. He used to take me to the cinema; we always watched Charlie Chaplin movies. My father really loved life as it was. He wasn't a rich man, but he made do.

My mother was always complaining about money. My father wanted to live day to day. Everybody in Iraq lived life this way, especially the Assyrian people. They were discriminated against. That's how the government wanted it to be.

After years of travelling everywhere, my father finally settled down in Baghdad. He wanted to be near us so he could look after his family. He got a job at a prison called Abu Ghraib. It was the worse prison in Iraq. It's where all the torture and hangings happened. My father used to work there fixing all the pipes and taps that didn't work.

I remember my father telling me lots of stories of things he saw in that prison—about all the prisoners there and why they were arrested. They would tell their stories to my father, maybe because they needed to release what was in their heart. I was bit older at the time, so I would spend time with my dad talking. When he used to drink, it's like he was letting it all out, telling me the stories of what he heard going on in prison.

In one of the stories he told me, there was a man who had been a general in the government of Iraq. He was a widower; his wife had died a long time ago. He had a daughter who was fifteen years old and in high school. He told my father how much he loved his daughter and tried to protect her from harm. He assumed that his daughter was going to school every day and that he had nothing to worry about. She was a good girl.

Months passed before one of the principals at the school called the father and asked, "What is happening with your daughter? Is she sick or has she dropped out of school?"

The father was very surprised at what the principal was asking. He said, "What are you talking about? My daughter has been going to school every day. I make sure she gets up every morning and gets dressed in her school uniform and goes off to school." He could not make out what was happening and where his daughter was going every morning and all day.

He did not ask his daughter what was going on. He had a gut feelings that his daughter was doing something wrong. One morning he followed her. She got to her friend's house and then both of them headed off, but not to school. When she got to her destination, it was a building he knew. There was a prostitute living in there, an older lady in her fifties, who used to recruit young girls to work for her.

He went into the building, and he was carrying a gun. He saw the lady at the desk and pretended to be one of the clients. The lady showed him the pictures of the girls who worked for her; their ages ranged from ten years old to twenty. He saw his daughter's picture in the album posing naked, and he said, "This is the girl I want to see." She gave him the number of the room his daughter was in. He hid the gun from the lady so she could not see it.

He went to his daughter's room, pulled the gun, and aimed it at his daughter. He didn't say anything to her, he just pulled the trigger and shot her in between her eyes. She died instantly. He went to the next room and shot her friend also the same way, and then the lady. After that, he called the police and told them what had happened.

The police took him in and questioned him. He admitted to killing his daughter for his honour, but because he killed two other people, he got the death penalty. He told my father, "Keep an eye on your daughters." But my father always gave us a lot of freedom. My father told me to always be honest with him and talk to him about anything on my mind, because it opened his mind more.

My father was always easy to talk to, unlike my mother. He always trusted me, but because I had so much respect for him, I just couldn't be open with him when I fell in love. He found out later on, but we still talked about it. Even though everyone went against me, my father said, "If you love this man, you can go and be with him." He was so understanding and respectful of my decision. He supported me even if it meant letting me go.

My father knew that if he let me go and I left the country, we might never see each other again. I did not think about that as a young girl of sixteen. I was in love, and all I wanted to do was to be with the man I loved. I had to let go of my father for the man I loved. If you ask me if I made the right decision, I do not know. All I know is that my faith had to take me on this journey. There was something I had to learn in this life, and oh boy, I learned so much.

Even though he did not have money, my father was a happy person. He never let the hardships of life get to him. If he had a dollar in his pocket, he would split it, half for himself and half for a person in need. He was always a giver, not a taker. He always helped others, no matter what the situation. My father was a kind and generous man. He always tried to do the right thing for his friends and his family. I am proud to be his daughter.

A Messenger from God

I believe that people who cross our paths may be sent by God. I call them angels on earth, walking among us. They talk like us and walk like us. They pretend to be like us, but when the time is right, they receive a message from God and pass it on to us. That's the only way God communicates.

You might ask: Why she is saying this? What does she know that I don't know? Years ago, when I gave birth to my second child and we were struggling financially, I was frustrated that I couldn't work because I had to look after my baby. I was praying to God every day. I needed answers to my prayers. I was very desperate and had so much pressure on me. I was trying to balance my finances, pay my bills, pay my rent … every day it seemed harder to survive.

It was hard for us, but I always had faith that God was looking after us. I never ever gave up. I was positive that things would change for me, my husband, and my kids. I did not know where my destiny was taking me. I had to have faith, keep going, and keep praying. I wasn't going to lose my faith.

I knew there was a test I had to go through. I felt God had plans for me. I just had to wait. Patience was the key. I also had this feeling that there were dark energy forces around me. I wasn't going to allow those forces to win.

This is a story about how God can answer your prayers every day when you are really talking to him directly. He will send you his messengers to give you the answers you need desperately in life. He knows what you want out of life and what you need, so he looks after you every day of your life. All you have to do is believe in him. The story I am about to tell you is so important to understanding what I mean. He works in his own way.

It started when my second child was one year old. My second husband and I were looking for work. We were very frustrated with each other. We had to find a way to make money. A friend of my husband had an opportunity for us to work in his business and make it successful.

I used to go every morning. I opened the shop, and every day, not many customers would come in. Things were getting worse and worse for us. Every day when I was driving, I was also praying to God to guide me. *What should I do to improve my life, and why is this happening to me?* I wondered if God was punishing me or only trying to make me stronger to prepare me for something better.

One day when I was sitting behind the counter, a man walked in the shop. He was not browsing; he just came straight at me. He was wearing a turban on his head, and he looked like a holy man. He was carrying a bag with him.

I thought he was a customer, so I said to him, "Can I help you?"

He said to me, "I'm here to help you."

I said, "What are you talking about?"

He said, "You have been asking for God's help every day, and you are angry with him. You think he's not listening to you, has abandoned you, and is not looking after you. But he is listening to your prayers every day."

I was very shocked speechless. I felt shivers run down my spine. I started thinking, *Who is this man, and what does he want from me?*

He said to me, "I'm here for you. I need to do a psychic reading."

I said, "No, I'm sorry. Thank you. I do not need a reading."

He persisted, and I said, "How much?" He told me it would be fifty dollars, and I said, "No, I'm sorry. I can't afford it."

He kept persisting and insisting on doing this reading for me. Finally, something inside of me said *do it, have the reading*, and I always follow my intuition. I said okay.

We sat across from each other, and then he said to me, "Take this piece of paper, and write down your favourite flowers and how many there are in your immediate family."

I said okay and started writing on that piece of paper what sort of flower I liked and how many people were in my family. He was writing at the same time. When we finished, we exchanged papers. I looked at his paper, and he had actually copied exactly how I wrote the words and the numbers. I was in shock. It was like magic. I could not believe it.

I said, "How did you do that?"

He said to me, "Do not worry about it," and he started to tell me that I pray every day to God and God did not seem to be answering my prayers. He said, "God is looking after you, but you can't see it just yet." He told me about lots of the things that were going on in my life at the time. That's when I felt protected by a higher power. I knew then I had a higher purpose: to accept my gift and help others.

Often we think that when bad things happen, we are being punished, but that is not true. These things only make us better and stronger. They help us believe there is more to life than what we can see clearly. We do not take things for granted.

We are only here for a short time. God gives us the willpower to choose the good or bad path. We have to channel ourselves and our energy into what's really important. We must know what we want and keep thinking positively no matter how bad the situation becomes. If something bad happens, then good things will happen also. They call it the universal balance; positive or negative, hot or cold, life is a balance. I'm still learning to channel myself, and I try to send good thoughts as much as I can.

I know it's hard to always have to try and never give up. Life is full of twists and turns, but you must have faith and continue your journey. Why rush? Take your time and listen to your intuition. Listen to your heart; it speaks the truth. Our minds can be very confusing, and that is how we lose our way. We find ourselves making the wrong decisions and mistakes, and we can't take them back. We have to live with them.

Look for the signs around you. I'm sure they are there for you to see. The answers are here on this earth, in this dimension. Be happy to guide others and teach the next generation so they can learn from our mistakes. We are writing the history we leave behind. I'm here now, and if I can leave something behind or teach people and guide them, that's what I am doing right now. I hope they will learn from me, become more spiritual, have more faith, and be open-minded. Anything is possible in this lifetime, because I learnt from someone like me. I'm just passing the message to the next generation.

Do Not Punish Yourself

We always punish ourselves for the mistakes we make. Why do we do that? We are only human. We are supposed to make mistakes in life. We don't think clearly enough before making a decision or saying a word we were not supposed to say. The past is a trap. The present is what you make of it. The future is unknown, because everything changes from one moment to another.

We are surrounded by evil. That's why we need faith to be strong. Faith will help you survive every day of your life, and you can face any obstacle that comes your way. God wants to reward you. But if you say, "I'm not worthy of this," then of course it will take longer for you to get your reward. Learn to accept and receive.